FEARLESS PURPOSE AND SIGNIFICANCE

Discovering How God Wired You
to Play a Role in His Story

by
Rick Adler

Becky may this bless your journey 's service to a deeper place with God. Rick

FEARLESS PURPOSE AND SIGNIFICANCE

The views and opinions expressed in this book are those of the author and do not necessarily reflect the official policy or position or Illumify Media Global.

Paperback ISBN: 978-1-949021-03-5
eBook ISBN: 978-1-949021-04-2

Printed in the United States of America

Contents

Foreword

RICK AND I MET SHORTLY after he took The CALL Vocational and Life Purpose Guide for the first time. He fascinated me with his executive ability to act with wisdom and his great understanding of various assessment tools. At the time he was leading a career transition ministry at his church and kicking off an executive and life coaching business. I actually called him out of the blue after looking at his results. What shocked me was his particular report contained a life purpose or calling-in-life statement. Let me explain: these were generated by the computer when he took The CALL. Part of the construct generates life purpose statements driven by each individual's results across their mix of gifts, interest, cognitive ability and personality and behavior traits. I took the liberty of calling him the moment his report was sent out to him.

What really got me when I read his was what it said: "My specific purpose in life is to serve others by coming alongside people to model Jesus Christ; encourage, mentor, and coach them to grow spiritually and glorify

Jesus." More amazing was here was a guy who according to all my data was doing exactly what he should be doing. This was a rare bird and I simply had to meet him. Most people who take The CALL do not know their gifts or their calling, or if they do, they are usually wrong. Rick was right on!

What began as an intellectual curiosity to me has blossomed beyond what either of us would have imagined that first early morning. He has continued to support my work and encourage and lead, because that is who he is, and I can use a dose of his coaching and managing now and again because he knows that is who I am. Along the way I have educated and honed his knowledge and usage of The CALL. In return he is a cheerleader in my life, helping me to navigate life and keeping me focused on developing The CALL 2.0. Besides all that is also a trusted friend and colleague.

Rick has used The CALL early on with the career transition group but since then with small groups of men he has mentored, with individual clients, and within organizations he serves. When he told me of his book idea and how he wanted to ambitiously explore some of the combinations of gifts and traits, I was impressed because it hadn't been done before. I am also incredibly passionate about people finding their calling and operating in life with God there, so any effort others extend to that end I support. *Fearless Purpose and Significance* represents Rick well, he lives in his significance with God, he does that on purpose with purpose because of how he is wired, and his journey has been an inspiration point for us to poke fun at each other and a demonstration of fearlessness.

As Rick often says to me, "What are you going to do now, what is your next step?" You can have that answer or not, but before you finish this book you'll be mapping out what God's next step is for you to live fearlessly with purpose, understanding your significance to him.

Enjoy and may God bless,

—Randy Austad
Author of *The CALL Vocational and Life Purpose Guide*

Acknowledgments

A BRIEF WORD OF acknowledgment to Randy Austad, author of The CALL Vocational and Life Purpose Guide, an online personality assessment. His tireless work for over a decade is part of the reason this book was possible. His purpose and significance is all over the work that he does, updating, teaching, doing more research about The CALL, while also supporting the people who take it or use it professionally. Randy is a remarkable man, and I am so appreciative of him. Randy is also gifted in teaching, so the veracity and validity of The CALL have made it a pleasure to use as a practitioner. All the praise for Randy and The CALL means that I never have any concern about the quality of the data or about the information contained in the various reports from the assessment, and can confidently use The CALL with family, clients, or entire organizations.

Thanks also to my wife, Marcie, for your love, prayers, support, and your gifts of knocking off my sharp edges.

Preface

I STARTED THIS BOOK over sixteen years ago. It began with the premise that Jesus was perfect; we will unpack that more later. Suffice it to say for now, this was not the average Sunday school definition of perfection. The project was to begin with exploring the personality and nature of Jesus like mapping the human genome. The concept was to explore Jesus' personality genome and determine within each piece of personality who he is and what perfection looks like.

At the time the vision was of a softball-sized diamond that a master jeweler cuts into a precious gem, with each cut revealing the stone's inner beauty, clarity, and uniqueness; the images of Jesus were to unfold the same way. Aha! Each cleft and cut could be measured, quantified, and analyzed so you and I could be "just like Jesus." After all, Scripture tells us that God is shaping us into being like his Son. So if I could map this out and describe what each facet of the gem looks like and represented, then you and I could simply live that out and be more like Jesus. "Sincy" was a code word between my father and I when I was in kindergarten, it meant "this will be easy, son, you can do it." Reading over my starting premise now, it strikes me as the thinking of that same kindergartener attempting to convey the cosmos. So several chapters into the endeavor the project was abandoned and lay forgotten by me until now. At the time the prospect of a self-help book to make you and me like Jesus seemed brilliant if only it were possible. Something felt off about it when pen hit the paper and the pages were typed out.

Since that day God has continued to work in moving and remarkable ways. I would never have imagined then what this book would have become. *Fearless Purpose and Significance* has moved well beyond marveling and discussing Jesus' perfection or a self-help book. To begin with "self-help" is not the correct approach to personal transformation. Paul calls us instead to live this way: "Therefore, my dear friends, as you have always obeyed— not only in my presence, but now much more in my absence—continue to work out your salvation with fear and trembling, for it is God who works in you to will and to act in order to fulfill his good purpose" (Philippians 2:12–13). The key to this passage is two words in Greek, *thelo* and *energo*. Thelo is translated "will" but encompasses desires and motivation, while energo means power or energy.[1] So we are to continue to walk in the work God is doing in us; he's supplying the motivation and desires with his power and energy. Whew, that is amazing and means much more to me today than when I first learned that passage thirty years ago.

Finally Os Guinness writes, "All who seek to follow Christ and to answer his call should pursue the key link between their giftedness and their calling, and use the best Christian books and tests on the subject."[2] So this book will attempt to cover that ambitious landscape beginning with Jesus, your purpose and significance to him, some insight I've gained from coaching the last decade, my transformational journey thus far, and my knowledge of The CALL assessment.

A Warning to Consider

Before you embark on turning another page, a few thoughts to consider. First, your exploration will be about who you are. Books always ask you to consider what the author is saying, to pause and reflect, but you are also being asked to ask God for his knowledge of you and together we'll explore that. Doing this is disruptive, and seeking God's voice while reading these pages will show you greater truth that he has for you. Disruptive is good in this case because God is the author of your life; it's his story, he loves you, and he alone holds the right to act any way he chooses.

Max Lucado puts it this way: "If we think that this life is all there is to life, then there is no interpretation of our problems, our pain, not even of our privileges. But everything changes when we open up to the possibility that God's story is really our story too."[3] This will change everything because we are inviting the author of the story into our story to edit it, make changes, and transform us into works of art versus a piece of work.

Erwin McManus urges us on with these words: "You have to know what matters; you have to know who you are; you have to know what your life is to be given to. For in the end, the one thing where you must never settle for less is the calling that God has on your life, the purpose for which he has created you, the impact he designed you to make in the world."[4] As the author, that is my heart too, that you know what matters, we explore with truth and science who you are so you can give your life over to God fearlessly, knowing your purpose and understanding your significance.

PART 1

JESUS AS THE GEMSTONE

CHAPTER 1

Jesus:
Perfect but So Much More

REGARDLESS OF THE PLUMB line or ruler used, Jesus has been held up throughout the church age as perfect. While equality with God was not something Jesus sought, we are told that he was tempted in every way yet without sin. So from the point of view of being sinless, he is like God. Here is where our discussion of perfection usually slows or halts altogether for several reasons. First, if we hold that Jesus is perfect, then our focus shifts to what Jesus didn't do. Second, focusing on perfection in the sense of what is done or not done divorces us from Jesus' humanity—his ability to negotiate life here on earth while living moment by moment in harmony with God—and from his consistent message about the kingdom of God being now. His fullness of life, exceptional love, splendid beauty, and perfection always delivered just what the moment or person needed. If we go deeper into the narrative accounts of the gospel, these characteristics leap off the page of every New Testament encounter.

But alas, our eyes tend to see the actions or things he didn't do. Jesus never drank too much, smoked, swore, lusted after another person, nor overate. We must stop short of saying he didn't hang out with folks who did do these things; on the contrary, these were the very people and places he preferred.

In fact, Jesus' first miracle, turning water into wine, demonstrates this fact. It was no non-alcoholic variety; it was the real stuff, considered "good wine." And wine without alcohol is as crazy as mixing a prized California merlot with a Kentucky bourbon on the rocks. In *Beautiful Outlaw* John Eldredge discusses Jesus' generosity with the wine and performs simple math to come to a whopping 908 bottles.[1]

Already our discussion of Jesus' perfection has drifted to the stories and his acts. Please forgive the digression, but if our focus is on what Jesus didn't do, at best we have lost well over half of who he was by not looking at what he did do. Furthermore, focusing on the dos and don'ts is not very helpful if our objective is to live a transformational life. Transformation requires change from the inside out, where our very fabric is altered and becomes something different based on the working stock God began with. So lest we forget Jesus is far greater than the things he did or did not do, we must recall his perfect life, his perfectly balanced personality and accomplishments, his unwavering obedience to God; we must remember that he is God's Son, the super glue that holds the entire cosmos together, our redeemer, and our all in all.

Back to the example of Jesus turning water to wine; whether this story is familiar or unfamiliar, so often these gospel accounts are either shrouded in myth or we just skim over them mindlessly nodding our heads. Either of these options robs us of the full flavor, of being able to notice the venue or examine the relationships of people in the story, which leaves us with a mere two-dimensional black-and-white picture of Jesus.

Unfortunately there is no depth, no multifaceted image, no color, length, width, or height; Jesus is just a black-and-white paper doll. My preference for naming this view is "binary Jesus," either a one or a two. There is no space in our puny brains for someone who is as multifaceted as a diamond. Most days we struggle with multitasking, and the prospect of holding two, three, or more thoughts all simultaneously at the front of our minds just isn't how we are wired. Furthermore, Jesus was navigating life here on earth always in balance with what God was doing, with what the people of the stories needed most, and intentionally moving the kingdom of God forward. Perfection just doesn't do this person justice. Our attempts at describing him all fall woefully short, anemic, and end up being little more than clothes on a paper doll.

Let's remember that Jesus was God here on earth: "For in Him all the fullness of Deity (the Godhead) dwells in bodily form [completely expressing the divine essence of God]" (Colossians 2:9 AMP). Jesus held the gifts of the spirit as exhibited in God his father but also equal measures of perfect love, peace, joy, and kindness. The hypothesis is Jesus navigated life with the gifts of the Holy Spirit, God's character, and personality in balance and full measure, which should bring us hope. Since Scripture says that we are being conformed into his likeness, that means that somehow God is transforming you and me so one day we will be like Jesus. Since Jesus was also fully human, there is some mystery to unlock about the human condition that will allow us also to be more "fully human" today. You see, we, not Jesus, are the black-and-white paper dolls, binary people. We are but a crude and misshapen likeness of a splendid, beautiful, and perfect God and a Son who is truly a chip off the old block. We live in two truths simultaneously, first Jesus' work on the cross makes us perfect before God the moment we accept his gift. The other important and comforting truth is God isn't done with us, he is also transforming us to be like his Son.

In *Beautiful Outlaw* John Eldredge highlights the fuller personality of Jesus by emphasizing the way the gospel stories reveal Jesus' playfulness, fierce intentionality, humanness, generosity, freedom, cunning, humility, trueness, and beauty. He also captures the shortcomings of calling Jesus perfect:

To say that Jesus is perfect—as the 'defenders of his glory' do—isn't the right choice of words. A stainless-steel ball is perfect; Cinderella's slipper was perfect; a haiku is perfect . . . His ability to live with all these qualities we've seen, in such a way that no one quality dominates—as is so often the case in our personalities—eclipsing the richness of the others. To live in such a way that there is always something of an element of surprise, and yet, however he acts turns out to be exactly what was needed in the moment. Oh, his brilliance shines through, but never blinding, never overbearing. He is not glistening white marble. He is the playfulness of creation, scandal and utter goodness, the generosity of the ocean and the ferocity of a thunderstorm; he is cunning as a snake and gentle like a whisper; the gladness of sunshine and the humility of a thirty-mile walk by foot on a dirt road. Reclining at a meal, laughing with friends, and then going to the cross.[2]

On one hand Jesus is just like you and me: human. At the same time, he is also much more complex than just a list of personality traits, gifts, strengths, or qualities. Jesus differs from us in how he always navigated life and walked in perfect rhythm to the Father's wishes. The people he touched, loved, corrected, healed, or drew near to were faced with encounters that were about much more than just love, perfection, or grace. Sometime his words seemed harsh, other times gentle and loving; at times he taught, whereas in other instances he attacked or defended. What I've begun to appreciate is that since Jesus was always in sync with God, he seamlessly adapted in each instance. He did this while demonstrating love, peace, joy, and kindness; the gifts of the spirit: prophecy, serving, teaching, encouraging, giving, leading, and mercy; and all the attributes John Eldredge highlights above plus so much more.

Remember how my original book idea so many years ago was to codify all this about Jesus so you and I could just run the program and become "like Jesus"? My hope is that you can see the fallacy in that type of thinking. It is important to admit we may have life with Jesus all wrong. To guard our hearts we must pray, "Jesus, when I slip into a performance mode or seek just to know about you instead of desiring a deeper relationship with you, please bring me back. If my obedience to you wavers because I've become cynical of being like you, encourage me, and when I lack faith, may you increase my faith and help me with my unbelief."

As I've mentioned, Jesus and his Father were in continual relationship, walking in perpetual conversation and connection. The good news for us is God desperately wants to do likewise with us. The goal is not to whip us up into some spiritual treadmill where our performance is measured out in compliance to some perfect list. Jesus prefers we just don't know *about* him but that we know *him*. His heart, his connections with his Father, and God's desire to show us how to walk in every moment of the day with him are far more than just the "knowing abouts" we could unearth. Besides, the best we could hope to attain are a few nuances of who Jesus is, and the deeper we move into this methodology-focused approach on just what he did or did not do, the more exhausted we become. Ultimately, this would leave us longing for a life filled with the real Jesus like a person gasping for oxygen. Our life would quickly be the first portion of Matthew 11:28–30 (MSG)—tired, worn out, burned out—versus what Jesus wants.

In these verses Jesus has this to say to us: "Are you tired? Worn out? Burned out on religion? Come to me. Get away with me and you'll recover your life. I'll show you how to take a real rest. Walk with me and work with me—watch how I do it. Learn the unforced rhythms of grace. I won't lay anything heavy or ill-fitting on you. Keep company with me and you'll learn to live freely and lightly" (Matthew 11:28–30 MSG). We were meant to live this way! Jesus showed us the way in the gospels and wants to show us still more today. Jesus did model perfection but oh so much more, and my hope is this book will aid you on your journey of being transformed by him.

CHAPTER 2

Abandoning the Yardsticks

DID YOU KNOW IN the business, psychology, executive coaching, and church worlds there are over seventy-four thousand different instruments used to assess personality types, thinking styles, emotional intelligence, talents and gifting, and vocational fits, to name just a few categories. The Gallup organization published a book based on the research of Don Clifton and Tom Raft, who focused on individuals' personal strengths and found thirty-four different traits. Named *StrengthsFinder 2.0* it has become one of the most popular books ever sold on Amazon.[1] There are other tools that focus on teams and team performance, 360-degree feedback processes for management, conflict resolution mode, and the list goes on and on. I might be considered an assessment junkie, both in taking them and attempting to understand myself in light of their results. I also creatively and actively guide clients, business associates, whole organizations, and friends to deeper levels of self-awareness and team performance through use and knowledge of these tools.

Like a good debate among Star Wars fans on which episode is best, I have personal likes, dislikes, and biases regarding assessments—which ones I think are the most accurate, complete, suited for specific purposes, or useful in leading people forward. Given this personal bent, how could we come to a chapter in my book calling us to "Abandoning the Yardsticks?" Simple: first, in chapter 1 the yardstick held up is Jesus, way beyond just being perfect in every way with many intangibles on top of gifts, aptitudes, characteristics, and attitudes. All the tools mentioned above have no category for someone so exceptional or fully functioning on all levels simultaneously all while being the most *human* human being of all.

Second, we do not measure up to Jesus, so measuring ourselves against him only reveals our imperfections. Third, measuring and understanding our degree of imperfection is also not helpful. Whether the comparison is to see how we measure up to others or pointing out what we need to change to be "more like Jesus," both are futile. Focusing in this way leaves us as slaves to what we do and don't do versus open to being transformed. Obedience is important in our relationship to God—Jesus demonstrated that—but our flesh and blood aren't reshaped by our actions alone. Fourth, many of us are predisposed to compare ourselves to others anyway, needing no encouragement to do so, and end up missing the point that the only standard for our lives is Jesus.

The final point regarding any of these assessments is that Jesus never took StrengthsFinder 2.0 (now called CliftonStrengths), Myers-Briggs, DISC, or any other assessment, so we have no way of validating what his scores would have been. At the end of our analysis we are left with Jesus being the perfect representation of God in human form with the full breadth of qualities, character traits, personality, gifting, and talents. This conclusion is not a bad place to land either.

As for us, God did not create man and woman flawed, warped, or lacking. While we were not equal to God, we were made in his image, and he called mankind "very good" after his creation (Genesis 1:31). Once the fall occurred, then the flaws, weaknesses, and shortcomings came crashing in and humanity started down a slippery slope revealing imperfections, flawed thinking, even lying. It took Adam only one question in this sinful state to throw both Eve and God under the bus. To paraphrase Genesis 3:12, Adam said, "I didn't sin; it was the woman you gave me." Thus, Adam was implicating God for creating a flawed helpmate (Eve), and it was their fault, not his own.

Hence, Jesus' scores wouldn't help us, but comparing myself to Jesus does reveal what I am being reshaped into: fully conforming to God's image and being fully human. Comparing myself to Jesus is also good when I think more highly of myself than I should. My strain of self-deception is that I do not always believe I am lacking anything. So seeing someone who is truly lacking nothing, namely Jesus, is helpful. Without a growing understanding of how Jesus navigated life and the accounts of his conversations, teachings, and encounters, the only mirror we might hold up is one to ourselves. Paul suggests in Romans that God's law also provided the same rubric, as if to say, "Here's Jesus, here is what one must do to be perfect." Then we fail repeatedly to meet the standard, and fundamentally this cycle will not stop until God is done with us and Jesus rights all things.

There is of course another camp of self-image. Many religious legalists hold that we are all just slightly higher than worms or pond scum, hopelessly entangled in a flawed body, mind, and spirit. Again true, in a relative sense: compared to Jesus, we do not measure up to God's standard.

Consider for a moment if all of us lined up at Long Beach, California, with the intention of swimming to Hawaii. Would it surprise any of us if we did not arrive? Certainly, some might make it to Catalina Island, perhaps a few beyond, but rest assured, most of us, myself included, would have drowned prior to leaving the protection of the harbor area. Creating a race to reenact this or some other way of quantifying our shortfall is not really helpful. Neither would swim lessons, really long measuring tapes to see how far we made it, or hula music played over loud speakers. Only a rescue boat, the Queen Mary anchored nearby, or an airplane to rescue us out of our mess would work. Then, following our rescue, we would need a means of transport to our destination. Jesus is the only way forward; he is both our rescue and our transport, the way and the life.

So each of us, whether we swim like Michael Phelps or dog-paddle like a toddler, must realize we need assistance to bridge the great distance and ultimately still fall short. As followers of Jesus, however, we should still desire to be like the One we follow. Perfection becomes the goal, not to measure up so we get into heaven but because we want to emulate Jesus in every way. What does it matter if either of us swims twice as far as our neighbor if we all end up drowning without knowing Jesus?

We have tossed around the notion of striving to be perfect like Jesus and concluded that is not the answer. Furthermore, using an assessment to direct our effort of being like Jesus is not the right approach either. This approach is more like plastic surgery; we are altering the features we see, sculpting them versus changing them from the inside out. Transformation is an inside-out process executed when we work with God. When we pull alongside his efforts and listen to his direction, in that process we become more malleable before him. A surgeon, on one hand, looks at a picture and uses techniques to change how you look. A physical trainer, on the other hand, leads you in a process that over time alters how your muscles work and how you advance toward your goal, ultimately leading to a change in appearance.

Several years ago, as a result of my own foolish abuse in my younger days of carrying backpacks for weeks at a time, my tendency to use improper techniques riding bikes, and various disease processes, I needed a new knee. Other techniques and treatments were no longer the answer, so a completely new joint was installed. Physical therapy was helpful, but it really couldn't stop there, though I'll confess for about a year it did. Fast-forward, I began working with a trainer at the gym. The very first thing we did was assess precisely what I was capable of, what my strengths were, what my weaknesses were, and what limitations I had.

The value of assessments is they provide data points about us, about who we are, our own relative strengths, weaknesses, and attributes. This knowledge, properly contextualized, is an essential part of our transformational journey. We must allow the truth contained in the results of these tools to illuminate areas where we are strong and successful and where there are gaps, deficiencies, and blind spots. Pointing out these strengths and weaknesses, which are much harder to discover by self-examination alone, is a unique feature of many assessments, and it is vital if we want to understand change from the inside out. Assessments also reveal interactions between the strong points and the weak points, and how they play off each other. Sometimes the greatest lessons and power come when harmony between traits exists, and other times the lessons revealed are in the tensions and conflicts in our hearts. The key here is seeing the data about us in the assessment results and then working from that point of knowledge.

Having this knowledge then should be paired with a few other components. Begin by asking God about what he sees; allow him to reveal prominent truths about you. This prayer may help: "Please illuminate what you would like me to know, today, tomorrow, and each day I walk with you, about myself and who you say I am. God, show me my purposes in service to you and how my wiring plays right into your story. Reveal those places of towering strength and points of tension and how you want to use me in both."

Recently I was moved one Sunday at church to seek out prayer regarding the point in my life where I found myself. When the pastor prayed, she paused then said, "I am not going to pray that your strong pride be removed, it is where this meets with a deep humility that you are driven deeper with God." God was saying in that moment that this point of tension in my hardwiring was valuable to him and my service to him. This was not the first time someone had highlighted this tug-of-war. I knew this one, but it was affirming and powerful in the context of the place I was at in life at that moment. It also provided Marcie, my wife and I a good laugh at my expense.

We need to remember that the mystery of self-discovery, as followers of Jesus, can be easier because his Spirit resides in our hearts. Therefore, getting to know God more deeply illuminates who we are. We seek to know him because he is the author and perfecter of our faith and because each step we take can make us both more human and more like him.

Besides increased self awareness and a deepening relationship with God the expertise of someone who can shed light on the personality assessment we're using and illuminate how to use it properly can facilitate us get the most out of our assessment. Selecting the best person is highly dependent on the assessment we select. We will discuss different assessments in the next chapter. The point is we need someone professionally associated with and experienced interpreting the tool selected. This can be a coach, counselor, or mentor, provided they have demonstrated success using the assessment we've chosen and knowledge of the tool's application.

Finally using these assessments also requires some reflective or meditative work prompted by thoughtful observations and questions. Often the assessment may provide some guidelines for reflecting on results. As a coach I prefer moving beyond the canned questions and providing ones specific to the person's results. This approach in my experience has demonstrated to be the best way to process the information. Having these questions in hand then allows you as the coachee or mentee to have a more intentional journey of self-discovery. A coach guiding your journey serves as a sounding board for what you learn and then suggest potential steps to aid in your personal transformation. Ensuring all four of these components are met assures you of having the greatest opportunity to grow, to gain a deeper sense about areas of personal transformation and connecting with what God would have you know from the assessment you've taken.

PART 2

WHICH IS THE RIGHT ASSESSMENT?

CHAPTER 3

Choosing the Right Self-Assessment

RECALL THAT THERE ARE over seventy-four thousand different assessments all competing for our attention, being used professionally, in schools and colleges, by businesses to measure suitability and fit, by laypeople and professionals to compare ourselves to the rest of the world and to determine where we rest on some cosmic bell-shaped curve. While I may be an assessment junkie, there are far too many types of assessments reflected in this broad range of applications and no single one is suited for everything, so we need to narrow the field. As we consider which assessment to put in our toolbox, let us pause to examine some key considerations.

Depending on our purpose or goals, different assessments are better suited to deliver specific direction and data. While it is instructive to learn about ourselves in terms of personality traits, intellectual or emotional intelligence, and other factors, we need a more holistic tool that will be more useful to our spiritual transformation journey. This allows us immediately to weed out certain tools. Likewise, tools that measure conflict resolution styles, our functional strengths and weaknesses, or the ways we interact personally or vocationally at work, without looking at spiritual gifting, do not paint a complete, integrated picture.

On the other hand, many churches or faith-based organizations have moved in an entirely different direction, motivated by the desire to see members increase their engagement with activities and serving within their church or ministry, so they may focus on assessments that only look at "Christian gifts," or what are sometimes referred to as motivational gifts. Again, however, this isn't a holistic approach either because there is often no mention of thinking style, personality, learning pace, or work preference. Work preference—in other words, what you are best suited for vocationally given your mix of personality attributes—is vital because for many of us work is where we spend our greatest chunk of time.

So we need an assessment that both focuses on spiritual gifts with an orientation of growing in our relationship with Christ but also recognizes our personality, vocational preferences, and learning style, and doesn't presuppose our vocation is inside the church full-time. To be sure, we should serve in small groups, community groups, and even larger home churches, but the majority of our time is spent either at work or at home. If our goal is personal transformation, the tools used will be holistic. Therefore, any assessment used for self-examination is relevant only if it is helpful in our homes and workplaces, where the greatest ministry investments should be made. Martin Luther recognized the importance of ministry in the home well before it was common for men to serve their families. During the Reformation, in reference to men caring for children and changing diapers, Luther said, "neither frost nor heat, neither drudgery nor labour, will distress or dissuade me, for I am certain that it is thus pleasing in thy [God's] sight."[1]

Nearly everyone in all walks of life has taken either StrengthsFinder 2.0, Myers-Briggs, DISC, or another similar assessment. Most of these strive to categorize us into our top five strengths or some mix of four-quadrant combinations. They are quick, have plenty of references and summaries, thus eliminating the need for expert diagnostics, and offer advice on how to relate to others. They are not holistic because they oversimplify personality and offer no key or insight into spiritual gifts.

Allow me to offer a couple of personal examples of assessments, their results, their proposed applications, and the differences among them depending on what your starting point is in terms of goals. The first example is the StrengthsFinder 2.0 assessment; at several junctions in my professional life as a manager or executive, I have used it to reveal my team's and my own relative strengths and weaknesses. After some discussion about confidentiality and of the data within the team, we took the assessment across all thirty-four strengths (or themes, as they are sometimes called). With everyone's reports in hand I then created a composite team report. What surfaced on both rounds for me personally were a couple of things. First, my top ten were slightly different between the two assessments driven by situational conditions in the organizations where I worked and the influences of significant life circumstances. What remained similar was one StrengthsFinder 2.0 theme at the bottom both times.

Using StrengthsFinder 2.0 methodology from the book the instruction is to focus on your top five and invest your time and energy there. As the author's theme and book title suggest, investing in weaknesses has a very low payback. The focus is to find your strengths and maximize them. I have several problems with this approach in general. Sometimes things at the bottom of the list (i.e., your areas of weakness) are career limiting and some strategy must be in place to mitigate them. Secondly, this assessment lacks any mention of spiritual gifts or personality traits, which are vital to consider if your goal is total transformation. Knowing from my from StrengthsFinder 2.0 results that WOO (winning others over) is at the top of my list of strengths does not give me a foundation for making me more like Jesus and living a transformational life.

Another example is The CALL, which I initially took over a decade ago. At the time, though I had been a Christian for over half my life, I had only done personality assessments similar to the four-quadrant types like DISC, StrengthsFinder 2.0, or church-led exercises about spiritual gifts. I was familiar with the seven gifts from Romans 12—serving, showing mercy, prophesying, leading, teaching, encouraging, and contributing—but never focused on them, didn't know where I had strengths or weaknesses, and wasn't really looking for spiritual transformation. Mainly I was curious and always interested in knowing more about my personality makeup and what insights The CALL might offer. So in this process I discovered strengths in leadership and encouraging but also very low scores in serving. In the world of statistics I was told my score in serving registered "well below the lower quartile threshold." This was a fancy way of saying it was in the lower 25 percent of the population, and my score hovered low within that group.

There was no arguing the results; examining my life and especially allowing others to do so for me, this truth resonated with everyone. An important side note: spouses are specifically good at confirming or denying assessment results, and I believe they are one of God's greatest tools in rounding off some of our sharpest edges. So I stunk at serving. I had known that God would like me to serve more, better, and perhaps from my heart and not from a sense of obligation. I can almost imagine God saying, "I would like you to be more like my Son, like a servant." In fact, Scripture supports this: "Many who are first will be last" (Matthew 19:30), and "Husbands, love your wives, just as Christ loved the Church and gave himself up for her" (Ephesians 5:25).

Since I took The CALL, I've viewed service differently, and one of my greatest acts of service has been vacuuming, both at home and even at one organization where I served as the COO. At home, due to a family health crisis, I performed this and many other acts of service in certain seasons of life as a full-time caregiver. This was so evident and transformational that a friend familiar with the results of my Call assessment almost always asks, "How's that service going?" or "Done any vacuuming lately?" As the COO for the organization I just mentioned, one of the daily chores was vacuuming the office, and because we were a small start-up and our staff had a variety of cognitive disabilities, janitorial work fell to me. One day an associate approached me and said he wanted to learn to vacuum because he had no other work to do that day. He said he had no idea how to vacuum, and when I asked him why he wanted to learn, his profound response was, "Leaders run the vacuum and I want to be a leader." Does God work in my life and those of others by operating from a point of weakness? You bet!

Don't get me wrong—I get jazzed, like all of us, doing what I am good at and operating from a position of strength; this is natural. Remember, God wired me as an encourager and leader, and is thrilled when I am in that zone and tight with him; that place becomes more natural to me each day. But equally powerful is the development that God has fostered in me the area of service one in me—put a vacuum in my hands and I need the power of God to get through it. The CALL continues to be instrumental in the transformational work God is doing in me. It has illuminated places where I know I need God's power and presence to operate, as well as areas of great gifting or power, but most of all getting to be more like Jesus in both these places spurs me on even more.

One other nuance is revealed in this example from my use of The CALL, that is, the beginning of a deeper appreciation for assessment results that enables deeper exploration of the interplay between these different aspects of who we are. How do encouraging and leading interact with serving or with other personality traits? As a professional, I have used every tool referenced above to serve clients, teams, mentees, family members, and myself with the goal of moving forward in life and work. However, from this point I will focus our attention on The CALL. Admittedly, there is no be-all and end-all, no perfect solution, but we can put a flag in the ground. I believe The CALL is a unique tool because it provides analysis blending Christian gifts in combination with interests, thinking styles, and relational tendencies all with an orientation toward vocation.

The CALL is divided into four broad areas, or categories, with some additional breakouts within each area. The four categories are Gift Mix (or gifts), Interest Mix (or interests), Cognitive Ability (or cognitive abilities), and Personality and Behavioral Traits (or traits). Within the area of gifts are the seven spiritual gifts previously mentioned: prophesying, serving, teaching, encouraging, contributing, leading, and showing mercy. Within the interests category, we have creative, mechanical, people service, enterprising, technical, and financial/administrative, each highlighting the bent of our heart. Whether artists or CPAs, people often have some level of passion for the vocational area they've chosen, and this category highlights their preference and the relative intensities of the dominant one versus other interest.

When exploring the cognitive abilities category there are five subcategories: overall learning index, verbal skills, verbal reasoning, numeric ability, and numeric reasoning. The cognitive abilities rating is often called thinking style, perhaps a more accurate descriptor. It is not a judgment of how smart you are, i.e., your IQ, or in any way an assessment of a learning challenge or other diagnosis. The overall learning index is best characterized as a gallon jug: everyone has relatively similar capacities, yet some are wide-mouth jugs and others are narrow-mouth jugs. How fast we can fill a gallon jug is based on the size of the mouth given the same volume. Results then are not good or bad, just different, and should reflect a blend of both the verbal and numeric areas. With each subcategory there is a focus; verbal skills looks at vocabulary, and numeric ability is a similar functional scale based on understanding of mathematical calculations. Then for each subcategory there is a problem-solving piece; numerical reasoning refers to your ability to use math to express and solve problems—if so you a numbers person? Verbal reasoning rates your tendency to use words to express and solve challenges—are you a word person?

Finally, the last category in The CALL, Personality and Behavioral Traits (or traits), is comprised of nine subcategories. What is unique here is that all of these subcategories—energy, assertiveness, sociability, manageability, attitude, decisiveness, accommodating, independence, and objective judgment—are on a continuum, which means we can display a significant degree of polarity. Let us briefly look at one of the more familiar areas and reserve a deeper dive into these traits for chapters 9 and 10. Sociability's continuum has introverts on the far left and the far right on the curve are the extroverts. Every one of us then scores somewhere on this curve. So remember, in this context the combination of these nine traits can be low, mid-range, or high for any one trait, which leaves us with eighteen (nine times two) different potential results.

However, it isn't just ending up on one end of the spectrum that is important. God has wired into us these combinations along the spectrum. Think of it this way: in the 1980s I got a new stereo with a graphic equalizer. An equalizer broke apart the sound of music into different areas, not just bass or treble but a spectrum from high highs to low lows, and depending on the mix an entirely different sound came out of the speakers even for the same song. Now we can't move some slide bar or adjust our personality and behavioral traits, but God did when he made us. He was a personality DJ, and the way he made each of us is just slightly different from the way he made everyone else.

At the end of this chapter is a one-page summary titled Confidential "Whole Person" CALL Scores, which is requested after taking the assessment by asking for the Coach's Brief. When taking The CALL there are a number of different output formats that can be generated from your one use of the assessment. This single-page summary is one of those, and it allows you to see sample scores in each of the categories we just detailed above. In chapters 9 and 10 we will look at The CALL 299 Motivated Abilities Combination Report (a.k.a. the 299 Report), but there are others, ones keyed to vocational databases great for potential college curriculum concentration; another is targeted for your calling or purpose; and several job-fit and team roll-up reports also exist. Beyond using the 299 Report with this book, determining which report is best suited for your intended use will vary; please feel free to contact Follow Your Call, or me via my website, www.rickadlerandassociates. com/fearlesspurposeandsignificance.

My experience with any of the different reports generated from Follow Your Call has been great insight and consistency of results. As the author of The CALL, Randy Austad, proudly maintains, statistical reliability is critical when considering what tool or assessment to use. First is the number and diversity of participants to demonstrate a sufficient sample size and lack of bias based on any demographic factors. Second is consistency over multiple assessments to demonstrate repeatability; in order to make sure the proper questions are in the assessment, you want to make sure those taking the assessment repeatedly do not have different results. Finally, a distortion score related to just the participant's responses is at the very bottom of the summary below. High scores here translate to higher validity; low scores represent inconsistent responses to similar categories. Overall you can have high confidence in these assessment results for yourself or for others you are working with.

CONFIDENTIAL "Whole-Person" CALL Scores

prepared for:	Joe Sample	2/19/2005

A "Motivation/Ability" debriefing tool for use by a qualified Coach of The CALL

Motivational GIFT MIX/Life Purpose from Romans 12 (FEET/Pathway)

	Gift Mix Order	Mod	Sten	Std Dev
1	Serving…moved to be a friendly helper	8.78	10	1.31
2	Showing Mercy…moved to show compassion	6.90	7	0.32
3	Contributing…moved to build value	6.85	7	0.29
4	Encouraging…moved to uplift others	6.85	7	0.29
5	Prophesying…moved to communicate God's truth	6.55	8	0.13
6	Teaching…moved to explain the truth	5.55	5	(0.40)
7	Leading…moved to orchestrate	2.60	2	(1.96)

Motivational Activity INTEREST Mix (HEART/Preferences)

	Interest Mix Order	Mod	Sten	Std Dev
1	Financial/Administration…prefers accountabilty	7.93	7	0.99
2	Mechanical…prefers to see tangible results	7.72	9	0.86
3	People Service…prefers a people fix	7.48	8	0.72
4	Creative…prefers freedom of expression	5.53	5	(0.47)
5	Technical…prefers to know why	5.29	4	(0.62)
6	Enterprising…prefers sales & marketing	3.89	3	(1.47)

Cognitive Ability (HEAD/Thinking)

Factor	Sten	Score
Learning Index *is an average of the general learning scores*	8	HIGH
Verbal Skill *measures vocabulary*	9	HIGH
Verbal Reasoning *measures ability to reason with words*	10	HIGH
Numeric Ability *measures ability to work with numbers*	6	Moderate
Numeric Reasoning *measures ability to reason with numbers*	9	HIGH

Personality & Behavioral Traits (HANDS/preferences)---Habits of thought

1	*Energy/Focus*			
	Relaxed, easy going	87%	13%	Quicker, needs more stimulous

1	*Assertiveness (Confidence in expression)*			
	Low-key, avoids confrontation	89%	11%	Takes charge, speaks up

5	*Sociability (Preferences in social interactions)*			
	Inner-directed, introverted	56%	44%	Outer-directed, Extroverted

	Manageability (attitude towards rules)			9
	Free-thinking, open to change	19%	81%	Conventional, follows the system

	Attitude (Trust)			6
	Skeptical, seeks verification	45%	55%	Accepting, gives benefit of doubt

1	*Decisiveness (time needed to think things over)*			
	Studies options to get it right	88%	12%	Acts on limited information

	Accommodating (yielding to others)			6
	Not a groupie; can stand alone	44%	56%	Team-player, cooperative

1	*Independence (Whose agenda to follow?)*			
	Other-directed, follower	86%	14%	Self-directed, goal oriented

	Objective Judgment (gut instincts or facts?)			9
	Intuitive, sensitive, emotional	21%	79%	Logical, objective, business-like

9   Distortion   Follow Your Calling, 2010

CHAPTER 4

Our Purpose and Significance in God's Image

IN 2010 THE UNITED STATES and many other countries were beginning to emerge from an economic downturn; by some estimations the recession of 2008 was worse than the Great Depression of the 1920s. Many people experienced significant transitions in work, joblessness, lower pay and benefits; their personal finances suffered, and even at a macro level employers treated and viewed the people who worked for them as commodities. During this time in my career, I was focused on beginning an executive coaching practice. Several years into this, God was calling me to a significant change, and at the time I had no idea where it would lead. I could only tell there was a significant bend in the road and God was calling me to abandon what I had done for two years and wait on him to open a new door.

Up to that point much of my professional success had involved covering for business risk and having contingencies always ready. One day an impenetrable wall went up and the door I left the room from couldn't be reopened; later I would learn it was a barrier from God to prevent me from having a plan B. I was angry and disappointed in the people who had suddenly let me down, and I instantly went into mitigation mode. All of this played out in mere seconds as I sat at my computer, in less time than it took to compose this paragraph.

As I began to assemble my action plan, there was laughter, almost audible, in my office. It was God; he was laughing at me, not in a hurtful way but with a deep sense of love that washed over me, and I could not help but smile. As my angst melted away, I had the sense someone was pounding nails. Immediately, I knew God had put the wall there, and his words to me were, "I made you the way you are and love you, but don't you think I knew you'd have a contingency plan? So in case you don't remember, I have a Son who is a carpenter, so I had him nail the door shut behind you." The rest of this story is for another day, but our God knows us better than anyone—better than our spouses, parents, counselors, or coaches—and it doesn't matter what is happening in our lives; he deeply loves us and wants a real and personal relationship with us. God's sense of humor came out in his line about his "Son who is a carpenter." God was being himself and playful with me, which spoke volumes to me at the time. What God's joke was saying was, "Calm down, you are angry and I'm in this. Just relax and let's have a laugh at the joke. My point about this story is what I sensed that day and still remember today—we are each unique, loved, and significant to God, who wants to know and love each of us individually.

Let's first remember that a loving God made us how we are. Our gift mix is hardwired into the fabric of each of us. The extent to which our spiritual gifts are exhibited has much more to do with where we are in our personal journey with God than with which gifts we possess. But make no mistake: the wiring is in your DNA just like your eye color and blood type.

Another key piece to my story here and how God made each of us is the difference between being special or being significant. If my experience and my story are entirely unique and no one else has experienced, then I am special. It would suggest that God sees me as a cut above. Have the hairs on the back of your neck bristled at even the mention of this? To be special means just that. The moment you or anyone become special, someone else can't be; they are somehow lesser because they can't be special too. But as my own story and the experiences of people throughout the gospel stories show, we are significant. Much tragedy, harm, and even world tensions, and wars can be laid down at the feet of our understanding (or misunderstanding) the difference between being special versus being significant.

I am guilty, you are guilty, and our culture propagates the tendency for people to seek being considered special.

Everyone wants to be special; my adorable grandchildren may not beg to be called special, but it is in their DNA and mine too. However, the moment I claim I am special, it means somehow I am better than someone else, the other, and because I differentiate and place some higher level of esteem on myself versus another, I am left with the requisite that this other must therefore be treated as a lesser.

Unfortunately, there is no way around this idea: if I am special, then the assumption is anyone who isn't me is by definition not special like me. Special means "better, greater, or otherwise different from what is usual."[1] Inherent in this definition is the premise that we cannot all be special; while we may each strive to be better, we can't all be the best at the same thing at the same time. It's an exclusive club by default. This hideous distinction means my demographic group, country of origin, hair color, or athletic ability—you name it, makes me better than someone else based on some ambiguous scale. We hear such notions in every sports broadcast, for example, "She's a special athlete" or "His quick feet make him special." Our schools, youth sports programs, annual review processes in the workplace, net worth statements, media outlets, marketing programs, and even our hearts all construct systems to maintain our own specialness or that of some precious group. However, God never whispered to me, while he was chuckling that morning, that I was special. We err when we hold out that we or someone else is in a somehow superior category.

What God did whisper was that I was loved, understood, and made by him. So we are unique, he makes us that way, but we are also all of equal value in his eyes. We are all significant too. Unique *and* significant—these qualities are so magnificent that all of God's history has focused on undoing what the fall did. In the garden choosing to be like God, Adam and Eve left all of us ruined and out of touch with God. Therefore, God needed to repair and undo what the fall damaged, beginning with how we relate to him. He doesn't differentiate between people based on any classification we can dream up, for he made each of us unique. Not only did he make you; he also made those adorable grandchildren I just spoke about, tribal chiefs, the warriors, CEOs, mothers, and me and you. And he also says every one of us is significant. There is no one "special," but everyone is "significant."

He demonstrates this by inviting us into his sweeping story, his story of wooing and redeeming us and undoing the havoc of the fall. While his invitation is personal—"Behold, I stand at the door and knock" (Revelation 3:20 NASB)—it is also universal. He has no bias, only love and the assertion we are significant enough to have made the cross worth his while. When I grasp this view and have my heart brought into alignment with his, then everyone is my equal, no one is more worthy than another, and nowhere can I point and say I am better or special. The ramification of this is no one is worthy of the war we wage on one another while claiming some sort of specialness.

Shifting to our gifts and how we are made becomes an interesting discussion. The extent to which we exhibit strength and gifts depends on several things. First, the maturity of both the observed and observer has a bearing on what we see. How well we've honed our power of observation is vital. So the observer must see with God's eyes, have his insights and observe from that point view; it is a combination of our abilities to see and what the Spirit is revealing that provides unique insights into significance. My ability to see others accurately improves when I see within the context of using my gifts with a growing maturity, all in obedience to God. The observed are also best equipped and their gifts most evident as their journeys and relationships with God deepen.

Let's unpack this with an example straight from God's story. In Exodus 2, while Moses was still in Pharaoh's house, he already had the gifts of leadership and a strong bent toward justice. It was built into who he was, so regardless of how deep or shallow his relationship with God was, we are still going to see these traits in Moses. While grappling with his identity and in an uncertain place with God personally, Moses responds to the slave taskmaster out of a sense of justice and in his leadership capacity. Moses does this with little regard for God, and the result is he kills an Egyptian to defend another in Exodus 2:11–12.

Both the Israelites and the Egyptians look at Moses' actions, unconcerned about his future, gifts, or tendencies, only that he committed murder. Now, three or four thousand years later, we can look at the broader story, see young Moses and old Moses and the role of each in history and God's bigger story. We can see similarities in the traits that would prompt someone to do what Moses did as a youth (not justifying it) and understand the downside of an overused strength becoming a real liability. Again, I'm not ignoring or diminishing his crime, but we can pick up the story later after old Moses has spent forty years tending sheep. He has been humbled after killing a man, being exiled from Egypt, serving his wife's family, and caring for sheep. Lest we forget, sheep are pretty stupid as livestock go and continually need to be protected and bailed out of tight spots. One day in his old age, Moses is now walking with God and has developed a curiosity: "I will go over and see this strange sight—why the bush does not burn up" (Exodus 3:3). Leadership and justice still beat in his veins. This day Moses was a leader of sheep, a good shepherd, which sounds like the perfect training ground for a forty-year camping trip leading two million people.

When we pick up the story, old Moses has identical traits, but he is now in closer submission to God but still not perfect, as we see in Exodus 3 and 4 where he argues with God. Moses contends he isn't the right person to lead God's people and is so vehement that eventually God has to bring Aaron in to help Moses. Nonetheless, the many decades this narrative covers display Moses' gifts of leadership and justice, both before and after obedient submission to God. Moses continues to mature, which now allows him to lead millions of people, to be God's man with Pharaoh and the Israelites, to deliver over six hundred laws (including the ten commandments), and to rule a nation. We will pick up more of this rich story and amazing man a bit later.

While I can neither confirm nor deny it, by all appearances Moses also isn't really sold on his own gifts; remember, he argues with God about whom to send to Pharaoh see Exodus 3:11. In Moses' defense, do herding a few thousand sheep really compare to returning to the land where you are wanted for murder, confronting the most powerful person in the world, and then leading millions of Jews out from a life of slavery? God isn't dissuaded, so we pick up the dialogue in Exodus 3:13 where Moses then says "what is you name" which is equivalent to us saying "who do you think you are" or "who are you to ask this," as if to imply, "This is a big ask from someone I barely know." God replies, "'I am who I am' has sent me to you This is what you are to say to the Israelites: 'I am has sent me to you.'" Exodus 3:14.

Moses isn't done; in Exodus 4:10 he says, "Pardon your servant, Lord. I have never been eloquent, neither in the past nor since you have spoken to your servant. I am slow of speech and tongue." And finally he flat out digs his heels in Exodus 4:13: "Pardon your servant, Lord. Please send someone else."

Like Moses, we tend to argue with God about what we are up against with our circumstances. We are also often blinded to our own gifts, perhaps because they aren't obvious to us while we're tending the sheep in our lives and then at times we believe the lie that somehow God ran out of gifts. This lie suggests that when God finally got around to us in line, he simply didn't have any more gifts to give. Which really means God isn't who he said he was, and we are asking Moses' question of God wanting to know who God thinks he is?

Just in case any or all of these run through your mind or you believe this is the narrative of your story, there is really good news! First, God is on our side, and he wants us to know and enter his story. Second, Moses did some amazing things as he walked obediently with God. Not perfectly but certainly trending in obedience. So being obedient to God changes our lack of understanding and our inability to see our gifts, and just like Moses we don't need to be perfect. We also see that Moses later, in Exodus 18:13–15, began to understand his gift of justice at a deeper level and embrace it. There are additional implications to this story that we will pick up together later. Third, we can allow personal maturity and life experiences to shape us. Moses, either unwittingly or intentionally, perhaps a bit of both, allowed his experiences of being exiled from Egypt, tending sheep, and wandering in the desert to prepare him and shape him. And oh yeah, while he wandered, in his heart there was still this deep sense of injustice, concern, and desire to change things for his people. Little did Moses know that this would prepare him for that forty-year camping trip with a nation in tow.

While the use of The CALL does provide significant insight, especially when it is supplemented with coaching, to provide even deeper understanding of our gifts as we are being transformed by God, nothing, no amount of self-help, can come close to God's help in understanding ourselves. As Hebrews 5:8–9 explains, Jesus himself "learned obedience from what he suffered and, once made perfect, he became the source of eternal salvation for all who obey him." So as we suffer and continue to be obedient to God, our capabilities, capacities, and compositions as individuals are all moved in the direction of perfection if we allow it. Our gifts come into focus, like turning the lens of an old camera, and who we are, our significance and purpose, begin to be revealed through our gifts and character qualities. So pray this prayer: "Jesus, teach me to walk in obedience to you, not the legalistic pronouncements but you, serving and following you. As we do this together, show me more clearly how you made me, my gifts, and who I am and what role you want me to play in your grander story. And as we embark on this, please use me to draw others into the story."

No discussion of this subject would be complete without a word about the other team on the field. That is right, there are always opposing teams, and knowing Satan's tactics regarding the giftedness God gave you is important. Satan's greatest wish is that none of us come into a relationship with God, but if he fails to thwart this, his fallback position is that we never discover how we are hardwired to serve God's kingdom. Think about it: this is not a bad strategy if your goal is to enslave people, undermine God's work, and prevent the advancement of the kingdom. So if the unthinkable happens and you come to know Jesus, then if I'm Satan, I move to plan B. All I need to do is distract you from finding out what your gift is or cause you to question whether you even have one so that you never serve from your place of significance and purpose. Many trapped in this state never discover what makes them so amazing.

Yet all of us are amazing, we are made in the image of God, and hardwired into us are gifts, talents, and predispositions for all kinds of purposes and for advancement of the kingdom and impacting the world around us so others see their significance as well. Even my tendency to have a fallback position in my career is not unlike our Creator. God too had plan A in the garden, plan B with Abraham and Moses, and then his master plan with Jesus. One of the key differences between God's plan and mine are is he knows ahead of time. Plan A and B would not pan out, but instead they pointed to Jesus as the way for his redemptive master plan to work, and it was supposed to be that way all along.

Without knowing what our purpose is or how God creates us uniquely, most people just settle on a vocation or are just trying to get by. Those who don't know God and are in the dark about themselves often go with their hearts or simply drift along aimlessly through life. That's not to say these folks aren't amazing; God's DNA is in their wiring regardless of whether they know God or how they feel about him. Their predispositions may lead to serving up good to the world or they may follow Moses' early example, driven by how he was made but without submission or obedience to God, misusing his greatest strength and ultimately inflicting harm. This, friends, is the cosmic equivalent of being a skilled carpenter with only a hammer. With hammer in hand, all relationships and projects are approached as if they were nails. So often we find this one skill or gift, our hammering skills, and we foolishly treat everything like a nail, and we say, "I just need to pound harder." Honestly over using our hammer is often what we do to the people around us, especially those closest to us, or when the heat is on?

Let's not be adrift, in the dark about our gifts, or merely using our hammers.

PART 3

WHO ARE YOU?

CHAPTER 5

Who God Says You Are

WE PREVIOUSLY TOUCHED ON the point that you and I are significant. Often, however, we create gulfs among us—often leading to war, abuse, slavery, neglect, and all manner of sin—when our actions and attitudes betray hearts that believe others are below us and less significant. In contrast, when I deeply examine Jesus in the gospel stories, he always viewed people as significant, placed the truth of their value and needs above his, and in each moment, being in relationship with his Father, gave every individual precisely what love would demand and deliver. He never compromised love, truth, or his sense of himself or anyone else.

A quick examination of Jesus' encounter with the Samaritan woman at Jacob's well reveals a few things. First, as a first-century Jewish rabbi, Jesus was actually sacrificing his own reputation by entering this area. Avoiding the area required two to three extra days of travel, and it was the custom to avoid it every time a Jew traveled. Proximity left one considered unclean based on the period's religious law and a form of racism, because Samaritans were considered half-breeds. Jesus didn't stop there; he went right into town and encountered a woman, scandalous by all standards. Making matters even worse, this woman had a reputation, which we'll learn more about, so Jesus had intentionally entered Samaria and was talking with a woman of questionable reputation.

He neither skipped the visit nor showed disrespect or demeaned the woman when the banter began. She was shocked, even putting up a bit of a fight in the conversation, and the disciples were shocked to find Jesus talking with her. In his actions Jesus validated women, the other, and anyone of a questionable background, and ultimately risked his reputation more by staying for a few days. We need to ponder this encounter, not just regarding the grace he extended but also regarding the measure of grace we should therefore extend to others.

Many who aren't followers of Jesus have merely skimmed the stories of the gospel or may disagree with the assertion that Jesus went out of his way for the marginalized of his day. Actually he still goes out of his way for the marginalized today, but most of the confusion for nonbelievers comes from religion and religious people. Sometimes religious people are well meaning and other times way off about what Jesus would do. Recently a dear fellow follower of Jesus confessed her participation in trauma counseling because of the way other followers of Jesus had undone her life. Not the type of encounter Jesus had with people. Another loved one has experienced similar rejection from fellow Christians after contracting an incurable rare medical condition. On multiple occasions well-meaning folks have asked to pray and then asserted that healing was dependent on the recipient's faith. Those are not the examples I read in my gospel, such as the woman who was healed remotely without Jesus even seeing her after a relative asked him for healing. We are made in God's image, but like Moses earlier in his encounter with an Egyptian taskmaster, we often damage and injure others either with neglect, knee-jerk reactions, ignorance, or premeditated actions, often with the sense it is up to us to defend God. So our discussion of who we are must begin with our place in the cosmos. We are not the center of the universe and we are not God. God, by the way, is perfectly capable of defending himself.

In Exodus 3:14, God introduces himself as "I AM." He just is. God has no beginning or end; he is simply "I AM." We talk about ourselves based on our vocation, marital status, age, nationality, or some other criterion so people can classify us. God is "I AM." We look back in history to identify, clarify, and justify ourselves or lean into some unwritten future if there is greater hope. God is "I AM." The "I AM" is history, which includes the future but always in the context of "I AM" here and now in the moment.

Henri Nouwen speaks of our internal need always to be talking; he says we can't be silent because we are always replaying conversations in the past or preparing for ones in the future.[1] We struggle to be silent, and if for a moment we choose to live in the moment, there must be a drug present to get us through; it may be music streaming, sports talk radio, perhaps food, relationships, or a myriad of significantly harder drugs. There is nothing wrong with music or a good ball game, unless we never come down and practice silence with God.

"I AM" would be a good place to dwell, this moment, then the next, and next. He gets us, and therefore it isn't necessary to explain who he is, and likewise, as I draw my life from him, in this fashion I need to explain myself less. God says we are wonderfully and fearfully made in our mother's wombs (Psalm 139:13–14). We are loved, and he desires to be with us, to dine with us (a bit more intimate), and to be our bridegroom (even more intimate). The entirety of the Bible is how he is wooing us, shaping and transforming us, and expressing how significant we are, always in the context of who he is.

When God first crafted us in his image, he did several things. First, Adam was made, but part of "I AM" was lost in just the male persona and therefore Adam was not complete. God needed his feminine persona to be represented, so Eve was created from Adam's side, part Adam and created by God in "I AM's" image. All of creation God called "good" until he finished making

Adam, Eve, man, woman; then he declared it was "very good."

Now as God's story goes and history bears out, we turned in disobedience from God, hid from him, and committed the first murder. God created us in his image and we tarnished it. As I AM's story then races forward we see Abraham, the father of many nations, where God makes a covenant with him but pays for both sides of the agreement in Genesis 17. Repeatedly throughout the Old Testament, stories unfold with people turning in disobedience, hiding and taking life, then God paying the price for the agreement. At many of these turns there are consequences for the choices people make; no one gets off scot-free. However, God's story is always pressing forward, and eventually he prepares and pays the ultimate price with the death of his Son, Jesus, to reconcile us to him and keep his covenant.

When you and I declare who we are, it can be said our self-definitions are unimportant because the story is God's; the great "I AM" owns the story. Yet in the strangest plot twist ever imagined God has a part for us. What's even more startling is this isn't some random crowd scene where we are milling around in the background while the big stars strut their stuff. Nope, we are all significant characters. We are part of "I AM's" ensemble. The definition normally used to describe an ensemble is "a group of actors who work well together, with no one outshining the others."[2] In that definition there is significance, equality, and value placed on each cast member. No men versus women, no religious chasms, no nationalities, no red state versus blue—each of us is a member of "I AM's" sweeping panorama called history.

Let's make this more personal. In 2008, my executive coach stressed to me the importance of creating a personal purpose statement. At the time there were a variety of projects, career opportunities, and clients competing for my attention. Focus was at a premium, and she proposed that creating this statement would serve as a filter for my life. If an activity or task didn't fit within this statement, if it bounced off, pushed life in the wrong direction, or wasn't intentional, then the cord should be cut, so to speak. After some significant time investment on my part and that of my coach, eventually my purpose statement emerged: "As a significant character in a grand story I will have the personal and financial freedom to encourage others in realizing their purpose which will further reveal my own."

I AM has called me to enter the ensemble. My personal purpose statement reveals much: There is an author writing a grand and sweeping story, a love story, and it is God. I'm not special, but God does say each of us is significant and he has a part for each of us to play. Woven into my personal purpose statement are a few parameters around freedom that were and still are relevant and intentional about how I live. My finances in relation to God's story, my personal health choices, and so much more enter into the mix. My desire and design lie in connecting others to their purposes (drawing them into God's story), and as I act consistent with who God designed me to be, I am transformed by him and an enhanced understanding of who I am, my significance and purpose, is revealed.

Now, when I assess the landscape of my life, it isn't as grand as Moses leading two million people from captivity, but each of our stories is proportional to our faith journey with God and the roles he has for us. Since each of us is significant and a part of the ensemble, all we can say is, "I am not special but I am significant," which was the same for Moses, King David, and Martin Luther King Jr. Simply put we are made in God's image to be in the ensemble. Let's briefly look more closely at Moses' life to discover lessons there are for us regarding who God says we are.

Moses, as we previously discussed, possessed a God given sense of justice and the gift of leadership. This played out even before he was walking deeply with God. How did that work out for him? Not that well, if you recall the incident of murdering a slave taskmaster. Later in life, over forty years later, he is now in relationship with God, following him obediently and serving as God's instrument. He is operating with justice and leadership, now alongside God. Soon after Moses leads all of Israel out of Egypt, we see Moses with a deeper understanding of his gifts of justice and leadership as part of God's ensemble. Eventually Moses understands and is using his gift to

be judge of all disputes and settlements between people
(see Exodus 18:13–23). However, this quickly becomes
overwhelming, what I usually reference as an "overused
strength." Moses is blind to this; at least the text would
suggest that. In walks Jethro, his father-in-law, who shows
Moses how overusing his gifts of justice and leadership
isn't working.

A few key lessons for us emerge from this example. First,
overuse of any skill can leave us myopic, less effective, and
ultimately a strength can become a weakness. Balance and
moderation are keys to successfully navigating kingdom
life. Second is the key lesson of listening to godly counsel
and coaching. Back to our Exodus 18 passage, starting in
verse 13 we see Moses explaining how he serves as judge for
the people. Jethro asks, "What's going on here? Why are
you doing all this?" (Exodus 18:14 MSG), but Moses misses
the point again and explains his process of mediation to
Jethro, only now in greater detail and perhaps louder to
push for emphasis. Finally Jethro is more direct (questions
and being direct are both valuable for a coach or mentor)
and says, "This is no way to go about it" (Exodus 18:17
MSG), then continues to expound on why.

Jethro gives Moses a plan forward, and once executed
we see this story plays out such that Moses is more effective,
no longer overwhelmed and overall better off. And that
isn't all; everyone else is better off. Moses has presumably
built up future leaders and is sharing the growth experience
of watching others step into justice and leadership as well.

Similarly, you and I must seek counseling, mentoring, or coaching, and do whatever is necessary to get it—pray for it, pay for it, whatever it takes—because wisdom is priceless.

Besides seeking this wisdom, maintaining a focus on Jesus and praying this prayer can also be very helpful: "Jesus, as you and I walk together, show me more clearly how you made me, my gifts, who I am, and what role you want me to play in your grander story as part of your ensemble. And as we embark, walking together in more deeper intimacy, please use me to draw others into the story." This is also a great place to interject your personal purpose statement; be sure to pray through what God would have you write and what or whom he wants to have help you craft it. Just like Moses, we are all invited by God into our own transformation as we move, grow, deepen, and mature in our understanding and execution of who we are.

I find rereading my personal purpose statement is always good, but as I mulled over this chapter, a new idea from God filtered up, a truth I had lost. The way it was revealed was so striking that I shared it with some men in my small group. The principle is essential to answering the question, who does God say you are? I was performing a writing exercise in my office. Beforehand, I was attending to client matters and busily sending communications, and two or three hours blurred by with barely a sound, only a slight muffling from my headphones. This particular writing exercise was called "To Notice," and the purpose was to stop long enough to contemplate the last twenty-four hours and record three events and perhaps if possible a lesson from each. Two quick entries surfaced, but I needed three and suddenly the winning entry of the day came, the ticktock cadence of my father's wall clock. When I finally noticed the clock ticking, with a chime going off once in a while, it became loud, but only when I listened for it, tuned in, and expected to hear it. Prior to sitting and doing this exercise I never noticed the clock. It had been running in the background for several hours; as the seconds and minutes passed, hours were marked with a chime.

It occurred to me at that moment that I need to be silent, to hush up, to stop life and be in the moment, the swing of the pendulum, and listen. To hear God, because rarely will he scream over the noise or rattle us so we hear. I must train my ear, ask God, who jealously wants to answer this prayer: "Jesus, teach me to hear as you do." Oh, the rush God gets when we utter those words. I imagine him responding, "Gladly, my son, this will be work given the noise of the world and your heart, but I will train you to hear my voice." As John 10:4 tells us, "His sheep follow him because they know his voice." Jesus wants to be recognized and to tell us more of who he is, who we are in him, and all about our parts in the ensemble.

CHAPTER 6

How God Wired You

WHAT DOES IT MEAN when someone refers to the way we're wired? There are a number of ways to consider God's wiring. Early in the twentieth century, with the invention of telephones, an entire career path opened up called operators. These people sat at work stations each with a predetermined number of inbound and outbound telephone lines running into the building and ultimately their stations. As calls came in, their role was to route the lines so that each inbound call was connected with the person the caller was trying to reach. Today this "routing calls" function has long ago moved to computers.

Computers of course have wiring, though we recognize it by the term *circuitry*, which runs internally between various circuit boards, and depending on the configuration and components on a particular board, the wiring performs in certain ways, for example, depending on whether you are a video card or math processor. As

Intel advertises, different types of computer chips can offer different performance depending on what we want a device to do. So how we are wired is really an element of configuration. Like computers, we are wired to perform and function in different ways.

Let us to turn to Scripture for more understanding on how our wiring is designed. As Paul explains in Romans 12:4–8,

> For just as each of us has one body with many members, and these members do not all have the same function, so in Christ we, though many, form one body, and *each member belongs to all the others*. We have different gifts, *according to the grace given to each of us*. If your gift is prophesying, then prophesy *in accordance with your faith*; if it is serving, then serve; if it is teaching, then teach; if it is to encourage, then give encouragement; if it is giving, then give generously; if it is to lead, do it diligently; if it is to show mercy, do it cheerfully. (emphasis mine)

Before we move on, please note the three emphasized phrases in the passage above, which we'll develop more later but are important to note here.

God is so relational, I guess we shouldn't be amazed when we read "each member belongs to all the others" since the story is God's and it really isn't all about us. Who we are is ultimately best found in the context of each of us belonging to the other as part of God's ensemble. So who we are has to do with the awareness that we need everyone at the table; discussing creative and mechanical traits, for example, we see what a powerful combination it would be to have these folks in the same room or on the same team. Remember, as we unpack each of the categories of The CALL, all are designed to be in the ensemble.

C. S. Lewis, when discussing the death of a friend, noted it this way: "In each of my friends there is something that only some other friend can fully bring out. By myself I am not large enough to call the whole man into activity; I want other lights than my own to show all his facets. Now that Charles is dead, I shall never again see Ronald's reaction to a specifically Charoline joke. Far from having more of Ronald, having him 'to myself' now that Charles is away, I have less of Ronald."[1] This is a profound explanation of our purpose and significance wrapped up in our daily encounters with one another in a timeless dance, our respective lights illuminating one another. My light alone is diminished, as is yours. While we are required to stand alone and work alone from time to time, there is a bias in God's story toward being in an ensemble performing life together.

The other two emphasized phrases from the passage above are closely related: "according to the grace given to each of us" and "in accordance with your faith." If we go back to the examples of Moses, we see a relationship between how his gifts were used by God in proportion to the faith and depth of relationship Moses had with God. As Moses became closer to God, walking and in constant communication with him, he changed. Yes, he matured but not just chronologically; it was also in how his leadership moved up a couple of levels. Early in Moses' life, while he still lived with Pharaoh, his leadership resulted in murder; later, as a reluctant leader and sheep herder, he brought a nation out of Egypt; and finally he proudly served as judge over all of Israel. We want to notice that Moses and our gifts are better harnesses as we deepen our relationship with God but at the same time God is making these gifts stronger.

We have been looking at general principles of how we are each wired, the importance of our wiring in relationship with others and God, and how our faith and the grace given to us affect how strongly our gifts are seen or manifested. Now we are going to look at the individual characteristics assessed by The CALL, one by one. We need to get a beginning grasp of each one so when we look at some of the combinations of gifts, attributes, and characteristics we don't get lost.

The CALL's individual characteristics, as explained briefly in chapter 3, are divided into four top levels, or categories: gifts, interests, cognitive abilities, and traits. Each of these in turn are further broken down.

Considering the gifts category, the seven gifts are based on Romans 12.

- Prophesying—Sense of truth and boldness to share it, visions for specific situations or people, comfortable confronting someone, desire to speak truth and eliminate uncertainty or ambiguity.

- Serving—Volunteers, action oriented toward doing things for others, has developed a keen eye to see opportunities to help, doesn't mind menial tasks, and typically very comfortable in the background.

- Teaching—Intentionally pauses to instruct, notices teachable moments and wants to maximize impact, remains curious and inquisitive, seeks out input and knowledge, and can be very scholarly.

- Encouraging—Coaches/mentors, serves as cheerleader, enabler of forward progress, optimistic, desires to exhort, and finds positive side of situations.

- Contributing—Generosity, wise steward, value adder, creates wealth, shares with needy, giver, multiplies opportunities, wealth, and assets.

- Leading—Action oriented toward group situations, willingness to be up front, unafraid to own group's outcome, confident and rallies people around theme, cause, or course of action.

- Showing mercy—A sense of who's hurting and desire to come alongside, nurturing, gracious to others, gentle and kind to others, extends benefit of doubt and forgiveness more readily.[2]

There are several key points to reference before we delve into the other dimensions of The CALL. First, although we begin with our gifting, don't allow the mindset to creep in that gifts are primary in importance. God made all of us. The key is harnessing this knowledge to serve in God's ensemble, as he would have each of us do. That could be done in the context of the church, a nonprofit, or the mission field, which may or may not be our vocation. The vast majority of us will see these gifts used in our vocational choices in business, the arts, the service sector, health care, or stay-at-home parenting. Our Christian lives and vocational lives are woven together, and we should not view them as exclusive or disjointed; they are integrated.

Second, as we begin to discuss combinations of gifts, traits, or styles across our entire makeup, we will see this integration more plainly. Let's say someone's dominant gifting is contributing, which could be linked to a strong aptitude for numbers; this combination can be far more powerful than just one part of that person's makeup. The sum of who we are, like most things, is greater than any single component.

Third, we must again not stray from the fact that we are designed to serve in the ensemble, and as much as you or I would like to operate solely in those sweet spots where we feel most alive, God would still have me run a vacuum. Find that place for you and lean into it. A good friend with an ironic sense of humor once greeted me saying, "You sound particularly upbeat, you must be doing a lot of sweeping." It just happened to be true because we were hosting a party later in the day. So before we blow off his sense of humor or the fact that "upbeat" and "sweeping" were in the same sentence, let us each consider, "What would Jesus have me know about working from a place of weakness?" It is where he is strongest if we will allow him in.

It is also important not to confuse what I'm saying with focusing on weaknesses. The metaphor I borrow from Jesus is walking down a road that is narrow and the path can be hard to follow. What else do we know about roads? Typically there is a crown in the road, the high point, so as rains come, the water runs off in both directions. As the water runs, it reveals another feature: the ditches on both sides. So often, our struggle isn't just the narrow road; it is staying on the crown and not being washed into the ditch or wallowing there. We are fickle creatures, and we find it hard to stay out of the ditches and off the crown of the road. We can spend our lives looking at and focusing on the ditches—our weaknesses—just as merrily as we can camp out on our high points. Remember, Moses' overuse of justice and leadership caused him to drift from a place of strength to weakness. So what are we to do to avoid this bouncing back and forth?

Remember that we are all on a journey toward transformation. You and I haven't arrived yet. As such we will have brilliant days and ones where we struggle to move forward or out of the tangled ditch. And most importantly, walk this road with Jesus. Don't check in during your morning coffee and leave him in your study; travel and take him with you. It is sort of silly of us that we spend time in our morning devotion and then think Jesus stays there for the day. Only by walking with Jesus moment by moment will we learn to walk the narrow "crown" of the road. Then we can begin to have the ditches cleaned out and be strengthened in those areas, all the while walking in obedience so we won't see a strength become an overused crutch.

Back to unpacking The CALL, next we will explore the category of interests. Do not confuse interests with what your broader vocational or hobby interests are, or some aggregation of the entire assessment and determination of what your interests are. The interest mix contains six subcategories, which are divergent or different from one another. So the interest subcategory titled mechanical could be aligned with an engineer, solar panel installer, auto mechanic, or hundreds of other unique career paths. They will quickly solve mechanical programs and may seek out projects to leverage this interest. The key with the interest category is the big bucket of six.

The next interest subcategory is creative individuals who, as the name denotes, like expression in a myriad of creativity endeavors. It could be their dress and a flare for fashion; they may paint or do pottery, music, or writing, or find great joy in gardening or arranging flowers or cooking. Quickly before we dismiss this vocationally, creatives are a joy to work with, and innovation and problem solving can go to a whole new level. Often I would characterize these individuals as being outside of the box. The world creates these imaginary or sometimes real constructs, and most of us pass our day operating within these spheres, or boxes. So often the creative doesn't even know there is a box or they may feel very constrained by it. Feeding who they are often takes time in their favorite medium or doing things they perceive bring beauty to the environment or situation.

Mechanical individuals often have an intuitive sense for how things work or the ability to tear into something and just figure it out. Perhaps you are like this or know someone with this sense, and it is a marvel to watch. They could be a CAD operator, auto mechanic, homebuilder, or president of a hardware firm. I know one individual who has harnessed these skills in helping people with disabilities with prosthetics, braces, and solutions to mobility challenges. I'm struck by those I know in this group, for they are always wonderful to have on a team and their competence shines.

People service, another interest subcategory, is different in many regards from the gift of serving. They may or may not be operating in tandem. We are looking at interest mix, so someone could easily not be good at serving but be fully alive in public service, government, massage therapy, or health care. This might explain the number of brilliant doctors with only a mediocre bedside manner. Their interest is in serving the whole of mankind and harnessing their own intellect. Likewise, a politician could enter the arena to change a city, state, or country. When we match up one interest with other gifts, interests, cognitive abilities, and traits, this interest can take on very broad implications in its contribution to the ensemble.

When we consider the world of enterprising, words like entrepreneur should come to mind. The opening trailer graphics from *Game of Thrones*, with turning gears rising up to create kingdoms, or the old computer game SimCity, where you acquired resources and outfitted cities, represent the essence of these individuals. All the gears and pieces come together to create civilizations, enterprises, or, to coin a modern phrase, tribes. They are focused on this delivering something bigger than themselves. Often these folks may be entrepreneurs, but they could also be those unique people in the workplace who build teams, either loosely or formally, to serve the organization. Kingdom builders surround themselves with people they energize around a mission, purpose, or cause. Depending on other personal blends of skills, gifts, and attitudes, this could also be done as a solo-preneur vocationally building a service organization or tangible product.

Those with a technical interest gravitate toward science and fields that are data rich. These individuals may be the source of data by performing research and analyses of experiments, or they may be enthralled with the similar work of others. They are driven to deliver the nuggets of knowledge only gained from rigor and work associated with scouring the information and immersing themselves in their field. While people with this interest may seek solutions to improve productivity or reduce some process time, they are not oriented toward cutting corners, generally because the validity of the process used is as important as the outcome.

Finally in the interest category we come to financial or administrative interest. Similar to technical interest, people with this heart usually share an enthusiasm for data, but they are keenly pulled toward the organization of it. Many CPAs would fit into this realm, but also actuaries could easily find their interests highlighted here. The administrative piece is also very high on these individuals' radar, as they like business processes or other functions to perform fluidly without waste or drama.

Whether we are looking at one of The CALL's summary reports or longer vocational reports, following the interest category we come to the cognitive abilities category, or how your brain works. Here we look at overall learning index, verbal skills, verbal reasoning, numeric ability, and numeric reasoning. These are measures of whether you are a number or word thinker and how you use either language or numbers to solve problems based on which speaks most to you. Cognitive abilities are plotted on a bell-shaped curve with people at both ends of the spectrum; however, normally our capacities aren't grossly different. So our varying results in this category are not good or bad, just different.

It is incredibly important at this point to address what is characterized as special needs individuals. Our varied reactions to this phrase are shaped by society, personal experiences, the people we know, their stories, and the incredible array of special needs diagnoses. Let's return to what we know foundationally: all people are significant. Furthermore, having worked with a variety of people in this population, it is clear to me that they likewise have certain characteristics, strengths, and weaknesses. While cognitive diversity in the workplace and broader fabric of society is vital, we still underestimate the astounding benefits it brings as well. However, the expectation for 100 percent of society's ability to log on to a website and take an assessment is not realistic nor should it be considered demeaning to provide other alternatives. So ordinary self-assessments may or may not work universally with special needs individuals. Visual challenges alone may rob all of the ensemble by excluding certain individuals, so a verbal version may be needed. Bottom line, we need to come alongside them in a more creative fashion to determine their place in the ensemble. Whether someone is on the autism spectrum or has some other diagnosis, these same gifts, interests, cognitive abilities, and traits emerge.

The final section of almost every Call report hones in on what are broadly called personality and behavioral traits. These traits represent perhaps the most researched portion of The CALL, within the assessment industry and psychology as a whole; the nine subcategories are broadly accepted with literally millions of responses validating the questions used and their implications. What is unique about these nine is while they are scored on a continuum with a bell-shaped curve and a normal distribution along it, we recognize and name both ends of their respective spectrum. For the non-statisticians among us, which is most of us, normal distribution means the largest portion of any population is in the middle. So on a scale of 0 to 10, the majority of scores are in the 5 or 6 range. Then as we move on the graph away from the midline, 4 and 7 ranged scores decrease in frequency, fewer people in this case, and this trend continues so the graph looks like a profile of a bell. On the outer edges of our bell are 0 to 3 or 8 to 10, and those who are statisticians could talk about outliers and other interesting math facts. What is important to us is scores in these ranges demonstrate a strong bias toward the respective end they are on. The easiest way to understand this is to look at the continuum's ends, where the contrast is easier to see versus the middle where more blending occurs.

Taking the energy-focus continuum, for example, we can imagine or know people we consider to be on one end or the other. Ever have that coworker or friend who just can't sit still, and to focus and complete a task just escapes them (perhaps it is you). In extreme cases, before they even begin something, it seems, they are off to something new. On this energy side of the continuum, they are tireless and boundless. What often eludes these people is "landing the plane." At extremes they are completely comfortable with having the sky overhead filled with airplanes circling the runway. Flash to some apocalyptic movie scene with airplanes falling from the sky; this of course is the challenge—airplanes come down one way or another eventually, and the question is how safely that touchdown on planet earth will be.

Shifting to the other end of the energy-focus spectrum—focus—these individuals have the ability to rest in an activity and complete it. They can be singularly oriented and stay on task. Since we are looking at the end of each spectrum, it is important to recognize that these highly focused people want completion. They won't allow the sky to fill with circling planes; in fact, only one can take off and it must land before the next takes off.

Multitasking, or shifting between multiple projects for some allotted time, can be their personal challenge. Their focus prevents them from letting go and moving to the next agenda item.

Next in our list of traits is assertiveness, which is essentially a nice way of describing how confrontational someone is. Higher scores causes tension with those individuals at the lower end of this spectrum because the high score person wants to "assert" themselves. Highly assertive people want to lead, take charge, and dictate the content of discussions, meetings, agendas, and directions the group is headed. They usually have some predetermined destination or plan in mind. In the upper reaches of the scale, often this can be done without thought for the other person or people affected by their own actions. In extreme cases these are the people who only display concern for their own personal agendas. Good reflection and self-awareness can lead highly assertive individuals to become more aware of the needs of the other.

As a highly assertive person myself, in some instances I intentionally make sure I approach people evenhandedly. This intentional approach allows me to bend toward a win/win outcome. As is the case with every personality and behavioral trait, life, circumstances, and stress can heighten what our natural state response would look like. A real-life example with a disruptive life event just happened for me; it made me very stressed, and I am normally a highly assertive person. I snap, literally becoming emotional, irritable, often to the point where I am attempting the Obi-Wan Kenobi Jedi mind trick. In the first *Star Wars* movie, when confronted by Imperial Stormtroopers, Obi-Wan holds his hand up and by speaking controls their minds. That is only in movies, thankfully; dictating what the person I am talking with will do, think, and respond shouldn't and isn't going to happen. The takeaway for all of us is that when one of our scores is more extreme, we must stay rooted in God and the ensemble to help us with the proper usage of a skill at that time in tension with the competency to move forward.

When we look at the assertiveness continuum, people who had results to the far left (lower scores), will struggle with the need to confront or share their position, which can leave them with a sense of being robbed of autonomy or a diminished self-image. At a minimum it robs relationships and groups of these individuals' valuable input and contributions. The best advice for leaders on this end of the scale is to overcompensate. Like the highly assertive person being intentionally inclusive and throttling back, leaders of a less assertive nature will need to be deliberately overbearing in their own minds. When this is done in conjunction with other team members while being authentic and transparent about their approach, it can actually pull other relationships into the mix as part of the solution. This behavior approach isn't intended to correct some wrong but to allow work and life to be done better together.

Again, our premise is that all are significant, not just the person who exerts their will on others. Likewise, those not inclined to lead every encounter can gain competency and confidence in sharing and properly expressing themselves and their desires. It is important to gauge your starting point and know that the stronger your tendency toward one end or the other, the more intentional your behavior will need to be to balance your approach. Seeking Jesus' input and wisdom as well as counsel from family, coworkers, peers, direct reports, and coaches/mentors is invaluable for us on all of these continuums.

Sociability is typically expressed by the terms *introverted* and *extroverted* and sometimes *ambivert*, so let's examine this spectrum. Ambiverts rest in the middle of the curve, and rather than being middle-of-the-road or modal individuals who don't fit either descriptor, they possess a relatively even amount from both ends. Introverts generate rest and energy from being alone and doing more solitary pursuits. They are not likely to jump to their feet, raise their hands, or shout out an answer or solution. The approach they prefer is weighing the facts, considering the outcomes, and intentionally responding. Within the context of social interaction, they prefer small groups, deeper but fewer relationships than their more boisterous opposites, and can easily blend into the background.

At the opposite end are extroverts; they thrive in group situations, look forward to meeting new people, love crowds, are engaging, vocal, and energized by social interaction. They are generally quick to raise their hands, talkative, and sometimes unbridled; often they will talk over the introverts and ambiverts in the room. There is some astounding research showing the need for organizations and cultures to have this full spectrum of sociability. Like so many types of diversity, sociability is yet another to take into consideration. There are examples of extraordinarily great leadership all along the continuum of the sociability scale.

Next in the personality and behavioral traits category is manageability, where our focus will shift to the two characteristics at the ends of the continuum. In general, the more manageable someone is, represented by a higher score, the more compliant he or she will be to directions, rules, best practices, or essentially coloring within the lines. Please remember, there are no right or wrong answers, states of being, or approaches, and the keys are self-awareness, functioning within the ensemble, and understanding limitations due to yours or other people's results. Highly manageable people are not very likely to deviate from prescribed methods or tasks where those lower on the scale work out solutions with more autonomy and self-determination in what can and should be done. In some cases lower-scoring individuals may completely ignore rules, methods, or directions, or, if forced to comply, struggle with their compliance even if they do succumb to "following the rules."

The value of these individuals, regardless of their scores on the spectrum, is what they bring to our families, communities, businesses, and each of us personally. A great example came about in 2007 that illustrated this for me when a Six Sigma business improvement project completely changed an established business process for my team. A number of team members who were lower manageability, like myself, were happy and eager for change; often low manageability people like me live by the mantra "we don't need no stinking rules." The change doesn't even necessarily need to promise improvement; just the sense of greater autonomy is enough to get our juices going.

At the same time one other individual—we'll call her Sally—had been the highest performer under the old ways of doing things. Sally had both productivity and accuracy dialed in. She was highly manageable and always compliant and lived by the rules. Long story short, the new process left her feeling ambiguity about how to perform her work; it wasn't clearly defined for her because of the newness of the process, so she struggled with greater freedom and autonomy. Yet Sally had been the bedrock of this department, a pillar, and the disruptive nature of the change made performance a challenge for her. But organizations need these pillars, and if the focus was performance only and not people, Sally's value could have been lost.

Coaching and communications eventually allowed Sally to soar again, and the fact that she functioned highly within the new methods allowed this new way of working to become best practices and resulted in creating what is termed institutionalizing learning. Let me explain: Sally needed rules, and this required everyone to write them down, summarize, and establish a norm for how we did this particular activity. So the organization and institutions, develop an expertise and standardized way of working or behaving. Without Sally the lower manageability people would have sought out this new change just for change's sake disregarding the positive step forward. We need diversity in the ensemble.

In the event you are following along in either The CALL sample report or your own Call Report, next on the list of personality and behavioral traits is attitude, which I have reserved the next chapter to discuss separately. Now we will move to the decisiveness subcategory, which refers to how rapidly you can make decisions. You should be seeing a pattern emerge. There are high and low scores, not good or bad. Making quick decisions can be a very favorable thing, particularly if the individual possesses wisdom and experiences that inform the decision well. However, like all personality and behavioral traits, if other people don't temper a highly decisive individual's fast decision-making with communications or knowledge or if the team is all low decisive people, it can lead to tension. On the other hand, not coming to a decision can be detrimental or even disastrous because waiting too long can also lead to discord in the group or the decision being made for us by default.

The importance of this continuum, as with the others, is the mix with other factors, how the mix affects the way we navigate life, and where Jesus would have us move with him. He can call us to a life of faith that plays out over our lifetime, but within that story are points of decisiveness. Many of us on the outer edges of this range need to seek Jesus and good counsel to be more centric but always in obedience. Maybe you are Peter hopping out of the boat: make sure you ask Jesus, like Peter did, "Tell me to come to you on the water" (Matthew 14:28). Bottom line, only Peter asked to walk on water; it appeared others never considered this bold move, perhaps because they were low decisive individuals. In my case what Jesus has been teaching me is to ask before I step on the water, as I am highly decisive. Peter walking on the water is one of my favorite stories, and it wonderfully expresses the spectrum of decisiveness, telling some to get out of the boat and others to ask before leaping.

The next traits continuum, the accommodating subcategory, measures our willingness to stand alone, the need for peace amongst the group, and to what degree we'll bend to make the group happy. Very accommodating individuals will sacrifice their views and potentially personhood to maintain sameness or peace. People who aren't accommodating demonstrate a willingness to stand alone and ruffle a few feathers in the process. Think of this as a cooperation scale.

Independence, the next subcategory, is perhaps one of the more easily recognized traits. We all know the fiercely independent people high on this continuum, those who strike out on their own, maybe a solo-preneur, never satisfied with the status quo. These are the Steve Jobses of our world, innovating perhaps but certainly not following the crowd. On the other end with low independence there is a comfort and tranquility when things are defined, same, and stable, and these individuals operate comfortably at the direction of others. Safe to say, on this continuum Apple Computer needed both types of people.

Judgment, the next traits subcategory, and decisiveness work together; while decisiveness speaks to the speed of a decision, judgment looks at the quality, emotional charge, and clarity of thinking under stress. People at both ends of judgment are able to make great decisions and lead well. The challenge is in blindly operating without knowing the implications of how you behave. People high on the judgment continuum may appear more unflappable in crisis and can be great go-to people when something unravels. They also approach things very logically and, in the event they are highly decisive, can make a logical and quick decision with little thought for the emotional well-being of the relationships involved.

People on the lower end of the judgment continuum may exhibit concern and panic easier, responding with emotion, but they can also possess a higher sensitivity to the environment, mood, and seriousness of what is happening. In a very positive light they are like a service dog that alerts someone who is going to have a seizure or the canary in the cage of an old gold mine. These individuals alert the unflappable folks that there is a problem. Without their emotional counterparts high judgment people could walk into a burning building. The low judgment person needs his counterpart when the building is on fire to navigate a way out. A powerful team when working together.

Part of the wonder of God and his completeness is his ability to navigate history displaying every characteristic we've briefly touched on. Certainly he himself is more than the sum of these characteristics. But never think of yourself or your results to The CALL or any other assessment as an indictment of some great flaw or source of shame. Likewise, the flip side of that same coin are those of us who think more highly of ourselves than we ought to. The point God reveals about the body of Christ, his existence as the Trinity, and about each is us is that we need everyone in the ensemble playing their part, both ends and all in the middle. Do I have an amen?

The final area within the traits subcategory is attitude, but since it is a whole different breed, we'll save it for the next chapter.

CHAPTER 7

Attitude: A Different Animal

THERE IS A REASON that we broke out attitude; all the other personality and behavioral traits have definitions around the names we use for either end of the continuum. But attitude is a different animal, low and high attitude, good or bad attitude or any other binary view really does not represent the complexity of this unique trait. Furthermore, more harm than good comes with lumping any of us into some category; "oh you are high attitude" or "so sorry you are a bad attitude." This view does not help us understand or map anyway forward with God or his transformational journey.

Looking to The Cambridge Dictionary about attitude we read "the way you feel about something or someone, or a particular feeling or opinion."[1] The only thing we can really glean from this definition is that attitude just is, our ascribing a negative or positive spin is only an adjective for the noun attitude. More than any other dimension or trait in the personality and behavioral traits portion of The CALL, attitude is the most unique and that is because; unlike the other traits attitude is part DNA, part life circumstances, and part choice.

Let's first unpack how we see attitude show up in our lives. On one end of the scale this trait manifests itself as skepticism, lack of trust, and criticism, to name just a few tendencies. When someone's results are in the lower third of attitude scores, lower than three for our discussion, we see these characteristics become more pronounced, and skepticism can move to a critical orientation, faultfinding, need for proof, and heightened impatience. In many situations one might consider these as examples of a "bad" attitude, or the negative side of the ledger, and for the moment I can only reply that depends because we are only looking at the outward manifestation without any perspective on circumstances or choice.

The flip side, in the upper third of the scale, typically what we consider the positive side, we see a belief that things are moving in the right direction, positivity, energy, and a trust resulting in greater patience. Even given identical situations, individuals may display a different orientation and interpretation. Is this good or bad? Again, it can depend based on circumstances and choice. Let's also remember, there are no right or wrong answers. How do we make sense of this apparent contradiction and reconcile what our view should be of anyone's results, especially one's own?

The CALL shows our biases in attitude, but unlike other traits it is not purely our natural state. Our natural state is who we first were, the five-year-old self with a little age variation. Attitude is related to how we naturally respond to change, news, or transitions. Spend some time with a group of five-year-olds and you'll see different responses to the same thing. You may see bouncing-off-the-wall excitement with one child, another could be in tears, and the third is rolling their eyes. Attitude is our filter or gut take regarding the world around us.

So attitude takes the natural state but integrates two other influences to arrive at an overall result or bias. The second piece is the situational or circumstantial state in that moment. Now our three subjects are seven-year-olds and about to go on a field trip to the natural history museum. For one child, it was extraordinary because they love dinosaurs. Another is bored and rolls their eyes because they much prefer the zoo. The third is in tears, frightened because they remember getting separated from the class on the last field trip. These reactions might not even align with each of the respective five-year-olds' reactions above and could be complete role reversals due to various influences.

The final piece affecting attitude is choice. On September 11, 2001 I was with a group of business colleagues attending a full-day conference presented by business leader Stephen Covey. The lessons of that day still live with me, but the most amazing thing Mr. Covey shared that day was choice. Even while events were unfolding, he excused many people attending because circumstances, their jobs, family concerns, or any number of reasons necessitated them leaving. No shame in going and none in staying. Then he shared his decision. He explained to the audience that unlike Pavlov's dog we have a choice. Pavlov conducted a famous psychology experiment where he repeatedly rang a bell, and after each bell ringing he'd feed his dog. Over time the dog became conditioned, meaning it concluded that when the bell rang food was immediate, and then he salivated when he ate. Watch my lab-golden mix any day to see this experiment reproduced without a bell, the trigger is me moving to the pantry where the food and bowls are stored. Anyway eventually Pavlov could ring the bell, not even feed the dog, and it still salivated.

Mr. Covey said he was going to continue that day because the acts of terrorism were meant to stop us, make us do nothing, or paralyze us with fear and terror. But he was not Pavlov's dog; in between every stimulus and response, as human beings we can choose. His choice was to continue and not respond as his natural state or circumstantial state might otherwise have dictated.

So within the attitude trait is a blend of influences. How do each of these influences—DNA, situation, and choice—impact your results? DNA is perhaps the easiest, though I won't touch necessarily on the broad body of knowledge in neuroscience, as that's beyond our scope here. Suffice it to say, there is evidence of internal wiring in our brain that leans one way or another. For our purposes it is simply whether your natural orientation is suspicious and skeptical or trusting and accepting. Determining this is less important than the impact of the other two influencers.

Every situation or circumstance has components that we share and ones that are unique. One of the business training classes I teach is around personal resilience and how we navigate the transition curve. This program is built on the premise of change management. Allow me to unpack these ideas of personal resilience, transition curve and change management all relate. Every change, whether it is personal like a new haircut, hitting the lottery, or being diagnosed with cancer, or some sort of global change like global warming, war, or a new government in your country, affects individuals differently. The process everyone goes through for each change is the transition curve, also referred to as the grief cycle.

This is our shared portion; we don't get to choose whether we go through the transition curve. How quickly and how successfully we move through it is where we differ and what shapes our choices over time. When we run this class, we ask every individual to list small, medium, and large changes and post them up. Every time, this exercise produces disparity in results: one person lists a haircut as small, another as large. In the event you and I cut off half our hair, how we look will vary, small for me because I have little and it's short, but someone who has grown it for a long time or cultivated dreadlocks could be in mourning for weeks. A bit more seriously, one participant posted divorce as a small change. I personally can't imagine that but know family members and others for whom divorce wouldn't be as big of a deal; a different participant may have been married and divorced six times.

What about something positive? you might ask. If you won the lottery, the average response might be, "I can't believe I won." That is the first step of the grief cycle, denial, but how quickly we respond and go through the cycle is also affected. No sooner do I exclaim, "I can't believe it" and perhaps suddenly I'm all the way at the end of the grief cycle, commitment, figuring our I'll pay off my house or start a charity.

Notice one other thing here: in the eye of the beholder changes aren't really good or bad; experiences create resilience, which shapes the response. Resilience is like our key muscle group for dealing with change. The more stuff, good or bad, we go through, the stronger our resilience muscle. But what about the really bad things like cancer and incurable diseases? Let's go there now because thus far we haven't mentioned God's place in attitude except the implied involvement he has with our DNA.

Jesus' DNA was no different from ours, and we see denial expressed by God's own Son, so we will begin there. In Matthew 26:38 we read Jesus' words: "My soul is overwhelmed with sorrow to the point of death. Stay here and keep watch with me." Then in verse 39, he says, "My Father, if it is possible, may this cup be taken from me," and finally in verse 42, "My Father, if it is not possible for this cup to be taken away unless I drink it, may your will be done." This is the same stage we are at when we get that diagnosis we were afraid of. Denial is being overwhelmed, sorrowful, fearful, pleading with God, "Don't leave me!" We are distraught. The next phase of the transition curve is resistance, and it is exactly what it sounds like: "I don't like this and make it stop." Jesus is right there with us, having himself begged for the cup to be taken from him. Sounds a lot like, "Make it stop. This is a bad idea, God. Isn't there another way?"

No passage in all of Scripture allows us to be more fearless than this story. Understanding our purpose and significance is amazing but only if we can live fearlessly as well. This is how it is done. Jesus voices from his heart and DNA exactly how he feels when he bargains for another way because of the circumstances, then he demonstrations the final piece of attitude, choice! Jesus choses to live in submission to God when he utters "not as I will, but as you will" and then finally "may your will be done." This is deep reliance on God, brilliant self-coaching, and steadfast obedience, even to the point of death.

So attitude moves way beyond the optimist who says the glass is half full. Many of us, if we are honest and consider ourselves optimists, smugly stop there. We say, "At least I'm not a pessimist who sees the glass half empty."

We have it all wrong, though, because neither is right. Our mission as part of the ensemble is actually to splash life from our overflowing cups onto all we meet, fearlessly!

A Chinese Taoist philosopher is traditionally credited with writing the following parable long ago:

> There was a farmer whose horse ran away. That evening the neighbors gathered to commiserate with him since this was such bad luck. He said, "Maybe." The next day the horse returned, but brought with it six wild horses, and the neighbors came exclaiming at his good fortune. He said, "Maybe." And then, the following day, his son tried to saddle and ride one of the wild horses, was thrown, and broke his leg.
>
> Again the neighbors came to offer their sympathy for the misfortune. He said, "Maybe." The day after that, conscription officers came to the village to seize young men for the army, but because of the broken leg the farmer's son was rejected. When the neighbors came in to say how fortunately everything had turned out, he said, "Maybe."[2]

The point is one might assume that all of these events were either good or bad. The farmer's attitude could display a bias that was either negative or positive, but he didn't because each time, the story wasn't finished.

Let's look at a personal example. In 1997 over a course of a few months my wife Marcie tripped while playing tennis, another time couldn't run, and then when the family went ice skating, she struggled to keep up with me, historically the worse skater of the family. You could ask why did she keep trying, why didn't she seek help, or why didn't she realize something was wrong. Marcie and I still respond periodically with our sick sense of humor and will reply to one another regarding these questions, "Denial is a wonderful land" or "Everything is great in the land of denial." Her troubles continued and still do twenty-plus years later. Eventually we left the land of denial and started a four- or five-year stint of seeing doctors and specialists after these seemingly random troubles. Things progressed to a cane, then a walker, and ultimately more advanced mobility devices. Early in this process we encountered a friend at the supermarket, before we had the diagnosis of Marcie's rare disease. When we explained what was going on, he replied, "Well, that is certainly inconvenient," which was perhaps the most truthful thing anyone could say at the time. Like the fabled farmer's son with a broken leg, having a rare neurological disease is not something anyone would wish on another person.

What was interesting during this time was Marcie had a filmed interview for a sermon series on suffering in 2002. By all accounts, having some mysterious and rare neurological disease can't be good, can it? But her response about whether it was good or not was astounding: "Yeah, it is hard, but my husband and I feel back in love again as a result of this condition."

If anyone were to ask you, "Is Rick positive or optimistic?" the answer would be a resounding yes, Marcie perhaps even more so. But moving beyond our lives the bigger story of God is what Jesus would have us believe in. Our attitude, as with the glass neither half full nor half empty, should be different as his followers; for us, the glass is overflowing. Jesus said the cup is overflowing, so regardless of what is in the glass, there is always more. Like Marcie, our view ought to be that our cup is overflowing and I can trust Jesus to redeem all things. Redemption never equals the avoidance or lack of suffering. The promise is God will see us through. His effort and energy is focused on drawing you and me closer to him, and since he's conquered death, ultimately his efforts are getting us into that story line.

Ann Voskamp's book *One Thousand Gifts* invites us into a view that doesn't ignore pain and suffering, but challenges us also to look at all the gifts life has to offer— to begin to craft a list of things we are thankful for, the beauty we see around us, the glass-overflowing events in life that can transform our orientation and ultimately even deepen our faith.[3] My personal battle has raged and waged with the rise and fall of jobs, other significant medical challenges, family losses weighed and measured up by victories, dear friends from jobs in foreign countries, the beauty of returning to Colorado, and just last week meeting our fourth wonderful granddaughter. It is our choice how we view life, and unlike anything else about us, a heart of gratitude can shape our attitude. The key question is, what would Jesus' view be? It isn't just what would Jesus do but what would Jesus choose, which is much more interesting.

"Jesus, through life's ups and downs, please give me your eyes to see, give me the assurance of things unseen that you are working out in my life, and help me to craft a lengthy and bountiful list of gifts so I can be freed up to be more active in your story."

PART 4

WHAT'S THE WAY FORWARD?

CHAPTER 8

Understanding Alignment and Discord Using The CALL Reports

WE ARE ON AN ambitious quest for self-discovery; we are using The CALL as our road map about who we are and how we are hardwired. The CALL will be our personality assessment of choice in this quest because it also includes the spiritual gifts we each have. We want to use the best tool and companion information to gain significant ground in this quest. This is going to be a challenge, and as with most quests, only those who are fearless and persistent will be successful.

In the next two chapters we will build on our overview of the traits and characteristics we discussed thus far but will move beyond just a single category and begin to examine combinations of category results. If we combined The CALL's analysis of the seven spiritual gifts, six interest types, five cognitive abilities, and eighteen personality and behavioral traits, there would be 3,780 possible combinations of gifts, interests, abilities or traits. Generally I like the presence of large data sets, but large amounts of data can be overwhelming and not always useful. My objective then in the rest of this book is not to provide some exhaustive list or table of combinations. I tried that and got a brain cramp, and I doubt anyone would read the extra three hundred pages required for even a cursory examination. However, it is important to think about how your results in one category would interplay with another, how you can gain a good self-awareness of your wiring with these combinations, and then determine what to do with that knowledge in your transformation journey with Jesus toward living out your purpose.

At the end of this chapter are two charts for reference to aid our examination. First is the 299 Report from The CALL, and second is the Urgency/Rapport Matrix. The 299 Report provides a unique way to look at assessment results and can be generated as a special request after completing The CALL. Every 299 Report is unique to an individual, so Joe Sample's report, a fictitious individual, is included. If you have requested your report, by all means have it handy, particularly for this chapter and the next. As we look across the top of the 299 Report, vocational interests (a total of six: enterprising, people serving, financial, technical, mechanical, and creative) and spiritual gifts (seven from Romans 12: prophecy, serving, teaching, encouraging, contributing, leadership, and mercy are ranked from highest results on the left to lowest results on the right.

Along the left side of the 299 Report are the combinations of thinking styles (five each: learning pace, verbal skills and verbal reasoning, along with numeric ability and reasoning) and your nine personality and behavioral traits. These last nine categories are each scored on a continuum with a unique characteristic at each end, for example, introverted versus extroverted. As one might expect, if you scored high as an introvert, conversely your extrovert score would be low. Scores that are midstream, a 4.0 to 6.99, will be in the middle on both the top and left side and center of the chart; these scores are shaded in white here (green on your personal copy if you have it).

Finally, the low-intensity range is from 1 to 3.99 and is highlighted in darker gray (gold on the hard copy report); it runs along the lower section of the left column and right side across the top, and the intersections will occupy the lower-right portion of the chart. These will be the focus in chapter 10 on discord.

Unlike the 299 Report, which is unique to every individual, the Urgency/Rapport Matrix is a general reference displaying all behaviors and gifts. I've created this construct to aid us in our discussion and as a way to categorized each gift or trait. The specific gift or trait is graphed where it stands on its own; in a perfectly calm world, with only one gift or trait present, the matrix shows where it would land in regard to the axis.

In the Urgency/Rapport Matrix, each gift and trait is displayed on two key axes, Sense of Urgency and Need for Rapport. The points on the graph are only high- and low-intensity ranges for any characteristic, and top to bottom is the need for rapport or relationship. Rapport is defined as "a close and harmonious relationship in which the people or groups concerned understand each other's feelings or ideas and communicate well."[1] This is the drive present in any single trait or gift for deep meaningful relationship.

The traits or gifts above the midline suggest a strong preference for quantity, harmony, and presence of relationships. Those whose traits or gifts appear in the lower quadrants favor fewer relationships, function more in the absence of rapport, or while favoring fewer relationships want deeper ones in the case of lower sociability ratings. The shift from left to right on the axis is urgency, how time sensitive are the traits and gifts, and how prone to a more immediate action someone is based on the particular trait or gift. So, for example, the gift of leadership is to the right edge of this axis, which means I will do this now, no time to wait, let's take action and act from the particular gift or trait. Similarly, in implication but at the other extreme would be someone who is low decisive: there is no urgency, the driving force is making the right decision, and if that takes four times longer than the average decision time, these individuals don't concern themselves because time is not of the essence.

The CALL categories of interests and cognitive abilities are not included because they are much more dynamic and change situationally with your age, what vocation and stage of life you are currently in, and a host of other factors. Psychologists tell us certain parts of our brains generally diminish in effectiveness as we age and become a bit more rigid. For example, while I loved college calculus and did reasonably well in my twenties, bell-shaped curves and marginal cost curves are only of nominal interest now, so I'm not going to do these types of calculations.

As we embark on uncovering what it means to have alignment (or discord) internally among our gifts and behavioral traits, let me preface with three key points, which are meant to contextualize the joyful mystery of who you are and how wonderfully you're made. First, we were made to be in a deep and intimate relationship with God. God is relational, and at one point the Trinity was all that existed. So this relational component is key to our understanding of ourselves.

God wants a continual relationship with us, so he's hardwired all of us, regardless of our Call results, such that we need to seek him continually. Many of us don't recognize encounters with God or embark on plumbing the depths of exactly what a relationship with him means, but these failings are our barriers, not his. A short prayer will be helpful here: "Jesus, whether I fully understand or comprehend what is meant by going deep with you, I want that. I admit, too, that my faith wavers here. I am afraid and don't really want my life to be disrupted or exposed, or for light to shine in the darker corners. Help me with that, too, so that each hour and day I am deeper in love with you and my gratitude for your grace grows as I see your love and mercy even more powerfully."

Paul so eloquently says we should think about ourselves and the entire subject of self-examination "in accordance with the faith God has distributed to each of you" (Romans 12:3). Verse 6 then says our gifts are "according to the grace given to each of us." Paul understands that you and I are going to need a steady and growing supply of grace.

Next in understanding The CALL result combinations, our greatest places of alignment will be points where strong biases collaborate to elevate our overall impact. We'll explore that in more detail in the next chapter, but for now we must remember not to allow our greatest strengths to be overused to the point of weakness. Also let's remember, just because we are good at one thing doesn't necessarily mean that is what God would have you do at this moment. He may want me to sweep. But sweeping isn't all he would have me do. So whether we are neglecting areas where we are weak or overemphasizing points of strength, ultimately it isn't about us, it's about God, his story, and our part in it. Therefore, we must allow him to work through who we are!

That means an extroverted leader at times just needs to be quiet and in the background, and the introvert may need to stand up and talk. Acting from our greatest gifting and strength is where we are indeed most needed, but it should never be the singular point of our offering or else it can become a weakness. We are not being disingenuous or lacking character or integrity when we act in our unique areas of weakness as part of the ensemble. Remember the hammer and the nail, and let's each ask God, "What tool would you have me use?"

Vital to our view of our strengths and weaknesses are the words Paul heard from Jesus echoing through the ages: "My grace is enough; it's all you need. My strength comes into its own in your weakness. . . . It was a case of Christ's strength moving in on my weakness" (2 Corinthians 12:9–10 MSG). Paul is acknowledging Christ's power in him and operating from the point of his gifting—speaking truth, leading, and encouraging—but Jesus' greatest work is often in our "handicaps," as The Message calls our weaknesses (2 Corinthians 12:7 MSG).

Working for many years at M&M Mars was extraordinary, and one of the reasons was how they developed people; they wanted people to develop and grow so they'd be more valuable to the organization. They would often put us on projects or teams and sometimes even in divergent jobs to expand our competencies and knowledge. Long before M&M Mars, God was doing this sort of personnel development—getting us out of comfort zone, our area of strengths, in order to develop our weak areas.

I encounter people every week who are miserable in their jobs; as a result of either intentional or unintentional choices, they have moved far from their sweet spots. Often they are considering career changes, which should cause them to pause because the grass is not always greener on the other side of fence. Perhaps they zigged when they should have zagged, didn't act in obedience and took the promotion (or didn't take the promotion), failed or got fired.

By the way I confess I've made all of those mistakes. In the course of writing this book, God reminded me of one job I had where I was very successful yet all the while I was also a miserable whiner lamenting to God how hard it was. From the outside it looked good—lives were touched, business and careers advanced—but my heart was darkly untrusting of God. How much more would my impact for the ensemble have been had I remained faithful in the calling to this job.

The reason you are standing where you are today matters less than how you are going to allow God to bring forth the greatest redemption and in the process draw closer to him. This is grace! And you want to bask in this grace and step forward with God. Use your experiences to expand your competencies or expand God; that's what he wants you to do.

In the parable of the talents each servant had different circumstances and were given differing amounts. The entire point of the story is to use what you have, so allow

God to grow your capacity and bring greater internal alignment with who you are—without the rush to start a foundation or charity, be a CEO, or get married and raise six kids. Maybe he will call you to do these things—start that charity, become a CEO, or raise a family—but the pace he chooses is entirely dependent on his story, not ours.

I've seen seasons play out in my life over years. Moses spent forty years herding and another time resigned from a job prior to interviewing for another and then moved to a foreign country all in four weeks. So it might be immediate, like Elisha minding his own business plowing a field one moment and the next becoming a disciple of Elijah dubbed to be his successor (see 1 Kings 19:19-21). In another biblical account, Sarah's and Abraham's lives, in their old age, were altered after ninety years by the birth of their son, shaping history and nations for centuries to come.

Let Jesus know your heart, the burning you have, and give it to him, allowing his perfect plan and timing to come to fruition before you force things. The parable of the talents suggests that those who are faithful with a little will be given more to give and watch over; God wants us to grow into this. It can be a quick turn or his plan may be slower, but the author of life crafted all our stories uniquely, for life. This anonymous saying summarizes it well: "God writes extraordinary novels for those who play God's game."

My goal is to help you understand your Call results. Throughout this quest we'll examine additional common characteristics in light of one another with an eye toward those biases that have the most significant impact both by themselves or teamed up with other gifts or traits. My treatment of every combination of traits and gifts will be on our agreement there is no right or wrong here; each of us is made fearfully and wonderfully. In the event you get your results and think, "Oh, I'm flawed," or "Oh, this explains my craziness," or go to any other dark place, none of that is true. The old saying applies here: "God doesn't make junk." My experience working with all kinds of people is that these points of tension can be some of the most beautiful as long as they are understood and embraced.

So if your results show areas of tension or some sort of dark hole, it doesn't mean you can't be a leader, pastor, CEO, mom, or servant. It also doesn't mean you can be a physicist either just because you want to. There was a time I could navigate a physics equation, but later it was never in my wheelhouse as a vocation. We can't do whatever we want; that thinking is just as flawed as saying, "I am special."

Remember, my goal for this quest is for you to discover fearless purpose and significance, then spread that message to your children, family, coworkers, and the whole ensemble. You will do this by steering them toward God and allowing him to teach, inform, and instruct you on where, how, and what he wants you to do in the ensemble for his story.

Special CALL Briefing Sheet for Coaches

The CALL 299 Motivated Abilities Combination Chart

Prepared for: **Joe Sample** The CALL taken on: 1/2/2018

Intensity Ranking of Chart		13 Ranked Motivational Gifts, Bents and Interest												
High Intensity														
Average Intensity														
Low Intensity														
		Creative	Mechanical	Showing Mercy	Serving	People Service	Enterprising	Leading	Prophesying	Encouraging	Teaching	Technical	Contributing	Financial Admin
23 Ranked Abilities		9.10	8.70	8.60	6.20	5.90	5.60	5.54	4.90	4.76	4.37	3.89	3.83	3.72
Passionate - Low-side Obj. Judgement	9.62	18.72	18.32	18.22	15.82	15.52	15.22	15.16	14.52	14.38	13.99	13.51	13.45	13.34
Self Reliant - High-side Independence	9.00	18.10	17.70	17.60	15.20	14.90	14.60	14.54	13.90	13.76	13.37	12.89	12.83	12.72
Flexible - Low-side Manageability	8.99	18.09	17.69	17.59	15.19	14.89	14.59	14.53	13.89	13.75	13.36	12.88	12.82	12.71
Anxious - High-side Energy	8.76	17.86	17.46	17.36	14.96	14.66	14.36	14.30	13.66	13.52	13.13	12.65	12.59	12.48
Take Charge - High Decisive	8.72	17.82	17.42	17.32	14.92	14.62	14.32	14.26	13.62	13.48	13.09	12.61	12.55	12.44
Individualistic - High-side Accommodating	7.89	16.99	16.59	16.49	14.09	13.79	13.49	13.43	12.79	12.65	12.26	11.78	11.72	11.61
Outer-driven - High-side Socialility (Extrovert)	7.81	16.91	16.51	16.41	14.01	13.71	13.41	13.35	12.71	12.57	12.18	11.70	11.64	11.53
Competitive - High-side Assertive	6.95	16.05	15.65	15.55	13.15	12.85	12.55	12.49	11.85	11.71	11.32	10.84	10.78	10.67
Inquistive - Low-side Decisive	6.70	15.80	15.40	15.30	12.90	12.60	12.30	12.24	11.60	11.46	11.07	10.59	10.53	10.42
Verbal Skills	6.43	15.53	15.13	15.03	12.63	12.33	12.03	11.97	11.33	11.19	10.80	10.32	10.26	10.15
Numeric Reasoning	6.11	15.21	14.81	14.71	12.31	12.01	11.71	11.65	11.01	10.87	10.48	10.00	9.94	9.83
Verbal Reasoning	6.11	15.21	14.81	14.71	12.31	12.01	11.71	11.65	11.01	10.87	10.48	10.00	9.94	9.83
Accepting - High-side Attitude	5.79	14.89	14.49	14.39	11.99	11.69	11.39	11.33	10.69	10.55	10.16	9.68	9.62	9.51
Cooperative - Low-side Assertive	4.24	13.34	12.94	12.84	10.44	10.14	9.84	9.78	9.14	9.00	8.61	8.13	8.07	7.96
General Learner	3.77	12.87	12.47	12.37	9.97	9.67	9.37	9.31	8.67	8.53	8.14	7.66	7.60	7.49
Team Player - Low-side Accommodating	3.02	12.12	11.72	11.62	9.22	8.92	8.62	8.56	7.92	7.78	7.39	6.91	6.85	6.74
Inner Driven - Low-side Sociability (Introvert)	2.96	12.06	11.66	11.56	9.16	8.86	8.56	8.50	7.86	7.72	7.33	6.85	6.79	6.68
Relaxed - Low-side Energy	2.16	11.26	10.86	10.76	8.36	8.06	7.76	7.70	7.06	6.92	6.53	6.05	5.99	5.88
Cautious - Low-side Attitude	2.06	11.16	10.76	10.66	8.26	7.96	7.66	7.60	6.96	6.82	6.43	5.95	5.89	5.78
Structured - High-side Manageability	2.01	11.11	10.71	10.61	8.21	7.91	7.61	7.55	6.91	6.77	6.38	5.90	5.84	5.73
Persaudable - Low-side Independence	1.85	10.95	10.55	10.45	8.05	7.75	7.45	7.39	6.75	6.61	6.22	5.74	5.68	5.57
Unemotional - High-side Obj. Judgement	1.48	10.58	10.18	10.08	7.68	7.38	7.08	7.02	6.38	6.24	5.85	5.37	5.31	5.20

Urgency/Rapport Matrix

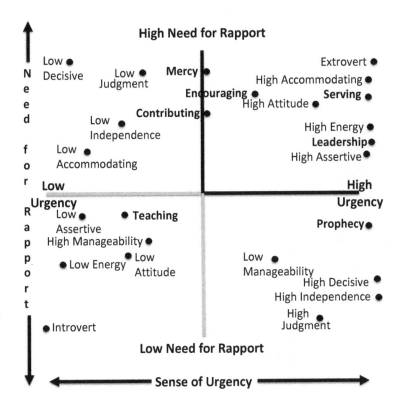

CHAPTER 9

Points of Alignment

THE BEAUTY OF A sunset, the majesty of a mountain landscape, the tones and composition of an orchestra piece—and I could go on—are all wonderful and inspiring because of the blending of some medium with another. The blending may be light and color, the alluring sounds of a group of woodwinds harmonizing, the stark contrast of snow and granite, or the funny hues, spots, and expressions of our dog named Pepper. Beauty is all around us; rarely do we think of the beauty coursing inside of us, but that is exactly what we are about to do. We are going to look at the wonder and beauty of who we are, how we are wired, and pay particular attention to those places where gifting along with personality and behavioral traits blend. These create contrast and offer up some unique compositions for our purpose and significance in the ensemble of God.

Leadership

Let's begin our look at spiritual gifts analysis with leadership. With those who score high in leadership, we know there is a natural giftedness to display urgency, take charge, take action, and lead a group. Thus, immediately we can generalize that urgency will be higher, further to the right of center on the Urgency/Rapport Matrix. Ordinarily someone gifted this way is not inclined to sit and wait for long, so gifts and traits that favor higher urgency can work in greater harmony. Those other gifts or traits in the upper-right quadrant of the Urgency/Rapport Matrix are like-minded with regards to time sensitivity. Whatever the key driver is for the other unique gift or trait, we will see a more immediate response. Extroverts engage meeting people, they are not the wallflowers; this leader will be comfortable being in front of people or engaging with a broader portion of the organization or community and will relish this role especially that of, wanting to get stuff done.

Adding the trait of assertiveness to the mix creates further buoyancy in confidence, and these leaders' strong competitive nature and readiness for action should bring victory in every situation in their minds. For individuals with these types of trait combinations, please be careful not to bite off too much, running out of steam in the midst of the endeavor, or running over followers or anyone else less assertiveness. High-energy people are always ready to bust out their next project or thought when they speak or take action. My type A genes love this approach, but as my wife has reminded me, you get more bees with honey, and honey is far more attractive than the stuff that attracts flies. Bottom line, don't overuse these traits; temper them with grace and seek God. Paul says to rely on God, encouraging us to "take captive every thought to make it obedient to Christ" (2 Corinthians 10:5). This is a powerful approach that will allow you to lead, take action, and move individuals, teams, or cultures in new directions.

The point for us to understand is if you have biased results in any one trait or gift in a particular quadrant on the Urgency/Rapport Matrix and another biased result for a second trait or gift resides there too, these mixes pull you in the same direction. This is true whether your combinations of greatest highs and lows in results are in the upper-right quadrant or one of the other three quadrants. Two quick cautions are worth mentioning again: with my combination of high assertive, high energy, and leadership I must remember that I am not a Jedi master and people won't immediately, or ever, just do what I say needs to be done the instant I say let's go conquer that mountain or whatever strikes that high-energy profile piece of me, living in that moment and always seeking something new. We also must remember that operating only out of these three all the time in every situation becomes an overused strength.

So having just stated that traits and gifts in the same quadrant of the Urgency/Rapport Matrix can pull with a shared strength in both rapport and urgency, with regards to leadership this means we should explore the gift of serving. Both are action oriented and prefer relationship, or rapport. This is a powerful combination for getting things done. If your combination expresses favor toward leadership you will be happiest up front leading and broader in scope, whereas expressions favoring service will be inclined to be in the background with a more practical focus because servants tend to think in that way.

Robert K. Greenleaf built an entire leadership model and modernized this approach in his essay pamphlet The Servant as Leader.[1] The amount of information, thought, and literature on the concept of servant leadership is staggering; concepts of filling people's buckets, operating at the pinnacle of leadership, or being a Level 5 leader are just a few examples. What is paramount, as Greenleaf laid out elegantly, is "The servant-leader is a servant first. It begins with the natural feeling that one wants to serve, to serve first."[2] From this point of view then, our leadership rises from within the heart and an orientation to serve institutions, communities, and teams, surrendering our own wants.

Greenleaf suggests that being encouraged or served by a leader is a powerful, life-altering experience for both the follower and the leader, and other books have been written as well about this experience. Many argue this was Jesus' approach and that he was the model servant-leader. I agree that this is the foundation of Jesus' leadership, but

I also believe he brought significantly more to his work on earth, referring back to the original premise of Jesus being perfectly well-rounded. Today more than ever in modern history few leadership models hold such promise in a world lacking true humility with other-focused leaders, thus making servant leadership my favorite approach.

My hope is you began to think differently about leading and serving. Let's do exactly the same exercise by looking at high assertive and leadership next. Using my previous personal example and my battle with being a Jedi master, this combination is eager to exercise control and lead the pack, powerful in submission to God. Gifting in encouraging and leadership also share a high rapport need but slightly less commonality with urgency. The encourager does not have to jump and immediately encourage like a leader, but rather takes the appropriate time to understand, then encourage, then lead. Hebrews 10:24 presses this point for everyone regarding the gift of encouraging: "let us consider how to stimulate one another to love and good deeds." Those gifted as leaders and encouragers can be more intentional, wanting to encourage others to follow and considering it an extreme joy to follow.

For the time being our last combination with leadership scores revealing a high bias with attitude. Those leaders with high attitude have a tremendously strong pull with both rapport and urgency because their attitude is positive right now. They trust that things will work out, people will come along because they get it, and the leader is there to rally them with the brimming confidence this combo brings.

Similar to our English language, where we have rules like "i before e except after c," we have discussed the gifts and traits that function according to the rules, those traits and gifts in the same quadrant as leadership that always harmonize. But high accommodating, mercy, and contributing are our exceptions here, and therefore we will discuss them later.

Serving

Serving, as we've said, has an orientation toward taking action but is content operating in obscurity as well as has a flare toward what is needed from a utilitarian point of view. The question for those strongest in serving is, "What can I practically do now for this person or organization?" As a spiritual gift contributing has a very similar practical orientation as serving. There are, however, some differences. Notice first that serving and contributing have a very different view toward the urgency. Serving is do it now, whatever the situational need it. Serving calls for action; contributing is looking longer term both from the time of action but also with a financial and practical standpoint. Contributing will take time to serve God's kingdom or other worthy organization or people financially. Those with a high need for rapport hold a similar strength as serving, encouraging, and contributing.

Serving blends with prophecy and teaching in the areas of sharing truth and knowledge with a heart of deep love for the person being served. While a teacher or prophet is content to share research and make sure someone understands or to share truth and call out incorrect thoughts, words, or deeds, people with these three spiritual gifts have the same desire to better someone in the exercising of their respective gifts.

Encouraging combined with service wants to help others serve the ensemble more completely. The server wants you to be unencumbered in pursuit of fulfilling your purpose, and the encourager is cheering you on in a specific way that speaks to you, your significance, and what God has shown them about you.

Mercy and serving mix well because both are higher on the rapport need scale, which means people are significant to individuals expressing either of these gifts. The server wants to meet immediate, physical needs, whereas those with the mercy gift have to have a target of their mercy. People with mercy are a heat-seeking missile seeking their target, where they ask, "How can I come alongside you and be the purveyor of Jesus' unending grace to you?" They desperately want to share with you a word or message to demonstrate how God's grace and love are functioning for you. Where these gifts differ is the sense of urgency: those with mercy are willing to be intentional and take time, but servers can't help themselves from jumping right in and saying let's do this now.

Contributing

Often there is a strong correlation between vocational interest and an aptitude for financial things. Contributing is the financial engine to the ensemble. While this gifting quietly operates behind the curtain, it is extraordinary what those with this gift will either do directly or position themselves to do long-term.

Several years ago I met a thirty-something man who had not yet identified contributing as his primary gift. As a young professional with three kids and a fourth on the way, both he and his wife were looking at "downsizing in order to be able to contribute more to the kingdom." Another woman has strong financial acumen along with the gift of contributing, so both of these individuals' traits and gifts, potentially even their interest mix, create a powerful pull in their lives to be contributors. Commonly this will even show up in a vocational orientation toward a career requiring good financial skills.

High independence and leadership can also further empower contributing. Highly independent individuals possess the ability to stand on their own and are typically self-motivated, making them a powerful ally because of this mix. Many times even the vocational interest to generate income or financial acumen and aptitudes for numeric ability and reasoning usually accompany contributing.

Practically speaking, if I am gifted to contribute, find ways to financially help, and exercise the gift, more powerful alignment will exist in other areas of my life. For example, leadership is manifested differently; if your scores are high in both contributing and leadership, it could mean you are the CEO of a nonprofit, a large contributor who gained a fortune as a CEO and now lives generously, or someone with strong financial skills that you harness to benefit others.

Prophecy

Any of you who remember the 1970s police drama *Dragnet* could easily quote the main character, Joe Friday's, mantra: "Give me the facts and only the facts."[3] Each week you could count on Joe, as some witness or perpetrator went rambling on, to utter those famous words. Joe was cold and factual, interested in truth and not warm fuzzies. Joe was a prophet: each week he'd tell them what happened, unemotionally with high decisiveness and logical judgment.

Joe also wasn't pushed around; he did what he knew needed to be done. That is because prophecy resides below the average on the rapport axis and is well to the right on urgency. The implications of where prophecy falls on the Urgency/Rapport Matrix means that the importance of rapport—the need to be liked, have lots of great relationships, and make people feel good—takes a back seat to truth. The prophet is most concerned with truth, sharing where the rest of us have deviated from the path of truth, and in a very pure and isolated sense is not concerned with the receiver of truth. Think back to the person with mercy being a heat-seeking missile for God's grace. The prophet is focused on truth and will defend it like a mother bear protects her cubs. Finally, because urgency is strong when the prophet knows the truth, it must be shared now.

Prophecy makes a powerful combination with teaching, leadership, mercy, and encouraging but each in very different ways due to differences in either urgency or rapport. People who are prophets and teachers will focus on content, not other people's feelings, because it's about knowledge and truth; therefore, there is often a point when these gifts are in tandem. But because of the difference in urgency, if prophecy and teaching are both strong, the tension will either create discord, next chapter's subject, or while disharmonious they can create a more appropriate response time. In other words, the teacher is patient and will take all day to make sure you thoroughly understand, and this will temper the prophet's high urgency around truth. This is a beautiful thing when these two gifts work tirelessly to share knowledge, make sure you get it, do the research, and wear truth boldly. It is God's desire these folks lean into each gift because he wants to leverage how he made us and our unique place in his ensemble.

Let's consider mercy combined with prophecy. In this case prophecy delivers truth and righteousness, and mercy delivers the grace of God wielded like a healing wand, bringing together situations and people. You can see this beautifully portrayed by Jesus. He had such a formidable combination of shining truth and then showing God's mercy by loving and extending grace to folks. An encounter in John 8 beautifully plays out this combination. It picks up one early morning; Jesus has left the Mount of Olives and returned to the Temple: "The teachers of the law and the Pharisees brought in a woman caught in adultery. They made her stand before the group and said to Jesus, 'Teacher, this woman was caught in the act of adultery. In the Law Moses commanded us to stone such women. Now what do you say?' They were using this question as a trap, in order to have a basis for accusing him" (John 8:3–6).

The "religious leaders" are attempting to trap Jesus, and hanging in the balance is only collateral damage in their minds—some woman (less than a man in their estimation) who is of ill repute (not nearly as righteous as they claim to be). But in Jesus' eyes she is significant. As John continues to narrate, "Jesus bent down and started to write on the ground with his finger" (John 8:6). What? Drawing on the ground? Really, what the heck? The religious leaders must have paused and thought to themselves, "We got him this time, he's speechless." The woman is clueless, frightened, and has no idea where this is going, but Jesus is distracting the crowd away from her, in my estimation, like a master illusionist with slight of hand. He says look over here where I'm drawing, and poof, the woman is gone. The net effect is now all eyes are on Jesus.

We pick up the account again a few verses later:

> When they kept on questioning him, he straightened up and said to them, "Let any one of you who is without sin be the first to throw a stone at her." Again he stooped down and wrote on the ground.

> At this, those who heard began to go away one at a time, the older ones first, until only Jesus was left, with the woman still standing there. Jesus straightened up and asked her, "Woman, where are they? Has no one condemned you?"

> "No one, sir," she said. "Then neither do I condemn you," Jesus declared. "Go now and leave your life of sin." (John 8:7–11)

There is no doubt in my mind Jesus knew precisely what this woman's lifestyle was like, and most portrayals would lead you to believe she was actually in the act of adultery and dragged out, presumably half-naked, into a crowd of predominantly angry, religious men. She would have been terrorized and scared to death. Then Jesus, holding all the gifts in perfection, draws in the dirt. Just for fun, when the time is right in heaven, I'll ask Jesus what he drew—stick figures, the Mona Lisa, who knows. But regardless of his doodling ability Jesus acts like a samurai, surgically wielding prophecy, mercy, prophecy, mercy.

The women knew the truth, Jesus knew the truth—prophecy with no words necessary. Jesus correctly chose mercy, and it was exercised perfectly by drawing in the sand. The focus is first on the woman scared to death and then all heads pivot to Jesus. Everyone is looking at him doodling in the sand. They are no longer looking at the sinful woman, half-naked—nope, all eyes are on Jesus. Then in a New York second, prophecy enters, and their heads snap from the woman to Jesus and then to their own feet, as he has them examining their own lives and the truth that they have sinned. Wham, the trap is sprung. Wow, what just happened?

One final swish of the sword—mercy—as he shows the woman forgiveness and sends her on her way. The heart springs open. Oh, to wield truth this way—sometimes it means the sword doesn't even need to leave the sheath—but here Jesus takes up mercy and prophecy so expertly with perfect love. My guess is this encounter was better for the woman than any scared straight program for juvenile delinquents at the local penitentiary, and it leaves the crowd speechless, as the prophecy was directed at the angry mob as well. Aspire to this wisdom and adeptness shown by Jesus, friends; I sure do.

Encouragement functions similarly on the rapport need scale as mercy, placing a higher value on relationships, and hence will combine with prophecy to use truth in tandem with desire to motivate. This combination can soften the blunt-force trauma of being hit in the head with truth because the spirit of encouragement is to lifting others up, sharing vision for how things can be, not just how they appear or are.

Teaching

Teaching resides in the lower-left quadrant of the Urgency/Rapport Matrix, displaying a low sense of urgency and a low need for rapport. Before we go deeper into teaching, this does not paint teaching as heartless or slow to respond. The focus of teaching as a gift is research, veracity of findings, and knowledge of the subject. Teachers have knowledge, which they have often invested their entire lives in, and they want us to walk through all the nuances of it. If it takes all day or a lifetime, teachers won't regard time—time to do the research, experiments, studies, and validation of all of their hypotheses. The teacher wants to bring us only the very best. The CALL as a body of work is precisely this. It is a life-time achievement with data integrity and veracity of truth, and its unwrapping could occupy volumes. Only a teacher could produce an assessment so complete. This is precisely the value. Because of how I am wired, teaching is number four, so I rely on the ensemble to provide other people to support what I do, and in turn I encourage them, my number one. You might say this is my paid political announcement.

All joking aside, this is the value of the different gifts and their importance in isolation but even more in their combinations found in you or me or within the ensemble of God's story. So when we look at someone with teaching as their primary orientation, words like methodical, intentional, and taking a process-oriented approach to disseminating knowledge come to mind. Therefore, when teaching is combined with low energy, in order to move forward get one thing done, take the time needed, then move on; for introverts, who quietly consider potential solutions or problems, often arrive at higher-quality responses that may require a bit more time than their vocal, extroverted opposites. In the case of low attitude combined with teachers, it can be mistaken for brooding or skeptical negativity, but really what we find with these folks is persistence and healthy skepticism. So together the teacher will take the time and even have a skeptical view of their findings, therefore painstakingly make sure the data is right before they pronounce the findings.

Teaching mixed with mercy is another unique and powerful combination. They are not really close to one another on either the urgency or rapport scale, in fact almost opposite, but what happens with this combination is there is such a heartfelt desire for other people to sense grace and mercy, and the validity and knowledge supporting it, that teachers with mercy will provide concrete and substantive information out of heartfelt compassion and love. Be warned, you will be overcome by someone with this combination and be so much richer for it. Don't get me wrong, for the individual there can be a healthy tension between the gifts too, one side wanting you to get it and the other loving you into getting it. Sign me up to spend the day with a teacher who is also strong in mercy. Most of us will walk away altered.

Encouraging

Encouraging is best characterized as having a high need for relationships, given there must be someone whom the encourager focuses their energy on and a moderately high urgency around that. Perhaps not as pressing as the leader's or server's time scale for taking action, there is still a bias toward offering the words, motivation, and encouragement now versus later. Teaching and encouraging can be nicely complementary to leadership. In cases where either encouraging and leadership are first and second in either order, people will potentially be more drawn to these individuals because they may appear more charismatic and knowledgeable. Encouragers will also see a heightened effect from gifts and traits located in the upper-right quadrant of the Urgency/Rapport Matrix. Certainly leadership, but also having high scores in decisiveness, energy, assertiveness, extroversion, and attitude, will accelerate and extenuate the expression of this gift of encouragement. Think about this notion of gift-trait combinations as leading to each gift or trait manifesting faster as a result of being encouraged and stroked a bit.

Mercy

Those with mercy at the top of gifting will have a synergy between being holy and kindhearted and compassionate. Clinically speaking, this definition is accurate, but what resonates when someone is operating from a merciful point is a heart with deep love that wells up and is inspired, straight from Jesus. In action, it is barely controllable and even the person's realistic view of individuals and the world are shaded with a brimming optimism and hope that sees from God's view.

Those operating in mercy strive to walk in humankind's our original glory, with a desire for holiness and a continual view of others with a healthy and godly duality. In this instance duality means holding two thoughts simultaneously; the person gifted with mercy sees in themselves and others displays of shortcomings from the fall, but at the same time senses Jesus' love and grace, and they express his mercy in every encounter. So when this gift is combined with leadership, encouragement, or prophecy, which are all more visible and overt, the combination is powerful and attractive to others. Like a hummingbird drawn to the promise of sweet nectar by the large Red King Humbert Canna Lily, we are captivated and drawn to the mercy of God.

Recently someone's gift of mercy was on full display encouraging me as a leader in my participation in an organizational consulting process. Ordinarily I might have been suspicious of being coyly manipulated, but the sincerity and purity of heart were unmistakable, and all I could do was say thank you and feel encouraged to be even more engaged in God's ensemble.

Low Urgency and High Rapport

The upper-left quadrant of the Urgency/Rapport Matrix does not, in a natural state, contain spiritual gifts. Nonetheless, as you'll see in just a moment, the traits here and their purpose in the ensemble are powerful. And remember each trait, unlike gifts, has a continuum with names for high and low range or intensity, and interestingly the lower results for decisiveness, judgment, independence, and accommodating all reside in this same quadrant. So the fact that no spiritual gift resides alongside these is not surprising because we are viewing each gift or trait in a purely stand-alone state and God knew when he created us each gift or trait would have modifying effects on others.

So the implication of that is that someone with the gift of mercy combined with low scores in accommodating would operate most naturally in this upper-left quadrant. Low accommodating in a sense pulls mercy further to the left, and we'd see someone living out being a team player and more supportive of group thinking from the low accommodating part of their behavior, while believing and hoping for the best with a dose of grace as a result of mercy. When I have led teams, these individuals are powerful players in holding the team together and smoothing out the ruffled feathers a highly assertive leader could create.

We should all remember that no single point on the matrix is representative of who we are. There is always a blend or combination in us, and as we pass through the day or our lives, in the bigger context situational influences will affect which trait or gift will be in the driver's seat and which one may be the passenger, providing navigation but not at the controls. So now let's continue our discussion of low results for decisiveness, judgment, and independence.

Someone who is low decisive will weigh information, the impact, emotional implications, and history prior to making a decision. In strong cases they still may not make a decision even after having 95 percent of the relevant information. The intention in this delayed response (especially delayed for someone who is highly decisive) is to preserve rapport. Yes, they may say, "I am slow at deciding, but I really want it to be the right decision for everyone." In the purest sense they want to preserve rapport, but what often happens over time is these delays actual erode relationships. The caution then for these low-decisive individuals is not to wait too long to make decisions.

The overall effect any one of these four traits—decisive, judgment, independence, and accommodating—could have in combination with characteristics like leadership, high energy, or prophecy, to name just a few, is very powerful. Consider the prophet's need to share truth, the urgency and push burning inside them, while tension could arise with someone who is low decisive: "Should I say it? Perhaps I should wait and get more information. The timing may not be right." Now if this is me and I turn to God and act in obedience, once the truth is uttered after that thoughtful deliberation, it could change the whole ensemble, or this chapter in the story of God may look very different from what we envisioned!

We've explored some common and powerful combinations of spiritual gifts and personality traits, those that produce harmony and alignment, and also synergies in the case of the last few examples. Last chapter we looked at each in pure isolation, but as I have reminded you, none of the gifts or traits are every truly isolated. We've also explored some examples of Jesus acting in his gifts, and these stories revealed that his gifts are perfectly woven like a tapestry. It may seem a bit messy on the back side, but when God turns it over and reveals the picture of Jesus' perfect work on earth, we all ooh and aah at the splendor.

Once you've taken The CALL assessment, look over your results. Our goal is personal transformation; we seek to fearlessly embrace how we are wired so that our purpose and significance are revealed.

Remember, we aren't special, but every person is significant. Remind yourself, your children, those you work with, and those who may report to you that our point isn't to steer folks away or toward some combinations over others but to steer them toward God. It is his story, and we are needed in the ensemble to deliver exactly what we were made to deliver. This prayer is meant to help all of us: "God, please the beauty and complexity of my combinations of gifts and traits, and show me the beauty of how I am made. What would you like to tell me about myself and why my unique combinations are so important to your ensemble and your broader story? Give me vision of how you want to use my gifts and traits. Finally, Jesus, teach me to fearlessly live out my purpose and significance today."

CHAPTER 10

Points of Discord

BEFORE LAUNCHING INTO THE topic of discord in The CALL results a brief definition will be helpful. Musically discord refers to a lack of harmony, and in relationships it is when people do not get along or agree. In regard to our traits or characteristics, again we are looking in a pure sense at one trait or gift coupled with another, both being in a natural state. Our natural state, as we discussed in chapter 7, is the reaction of each gift or trait in a five-year-old's state; so we look at a gift or trait in this state and then combine it with another in the same state. The challenge is these opposing forces are each simultaneously orchestrating a tune playing or force pulling inside us, so it becomes two tunes playing or forces pulling in opposite directions.

When we have these opposing gifts and traits, we lack harmony inside, and we struggle to act in integrity with ourselves. Depending on the strength of the bias in each gift or trait, the outcome can range from internal disagreement to outright tension, stress, or sickness. When we speak of integrity, this isn't our honesty or what we do when no one is watching; this is about internal consistency. Think of it like a tension that can arise between you and your spouse, friend, or boss, but in this case it is between you and you. You are at war with yourself because of this conflict, and the tension that exists must be dealt with. Even if you have been unaware of it, you need to see it, understand it, and then allow God to instruct you on how to navigate life in light of these points of discord and aid you in knowing mitigation methods and then leveraging these tensions.

It is important too not to stress, worry, or panic if two polar opposite traits or gifts bubble up on your results when you look at your 299 Report or the Urgency/Rapport Matrix. Remember also, if you see a score of 4 on one scale and a 6 on another, don't expect there will be a civil war inside you that will rip you apart until years of counseling and therapy get you untangled. Let's remember "that he who began a good work in you will carry it on to completion" (Philippians 1:6). So what seems like a beautiful/ugly at best is beautiful in his eyes, even as his redemptive powers transform you.

Prophecy

Prophecy and leadership together are a powerful combination. The net effect of these two pulling can also create discord, however. That's right, powerful and pulling potentially in opposite directions. These two gifts, like so many gifts and traits, can function like Doctor Doolittle's "push-me-pull-me," and you might struggle to move forward, to find clarity, and to learn how to leverage these natural tendencies. Specific to prophecy and leadership, a key to harnessing them successfully is understanding the drive to be up front, the tendency to share truth and insight, and the potential danger from those actions being unbridled. One has to have a tempered view of speaking the truth in love and taking a leadership position to move things forward, not just a pulpit to blast followers. Thus, we see the rapport need piece is significantly lower for the prophet.

The combination of prophecy and teaching is another place where we can sense this extreme tension. Teachers, as discussed earlier, want to emphasize the veracity of the research, the knowledge, and deliver it intentionally with little regard to time, while the prophet is striving to lay truth and rightness down now. The pull from both these gifts can leave you with an unexplained tension, feeling like "this is too hard" or "I'm not sure how to move forward," when you are presented with situations calling for either gift to step up. However, when harnessed by God—after all, he did your wiring—the dampening effect can lead to even greater effectiveness in the ensemble actually where the sum of these gifts is greater than just the one.

In the last chapter we talked about mercy and prophecy shown together in Jesus' dealing with the woman caught in adultery. We focused in on Jesus' adeptness in using the two gifts in tandem, but foundationally you and I are nowhere near where Jesus was in personal transformation. Mercy is patience and focused on grace, prophecy on truth with a strong sense urgency around righteousness. This can create a very challenging scenario to navigate life with.

While Jesus is one example of this combo done well, people who possess these two gifts as numbers one and two demonstrate a struggle. What emerges for thousands of people with these Call results is a segment of culture that either remains alone or feels that way and is challenged to find lasting relationships. Often they are drawn to troubled people, either in dating or marriage relationships, where the other person is deeply flawed. The merciful portion is drawn in desiring restoration, grace, and love, but then the prophet wants to flee because of the need for righteousness and the ability to see truth in the relationship and the flawed nature of the other person. Perhaps after some time the relationship ends, but reestablishing a new marriage is hard because the prophet seeks a saint worthy of investment. When someone's faith grows and they deepen their life with God regarding their gifting in these areas, this often leads to lasting marriages. This is the resultant effect of God being at work, the individual's growth yielded to what God is doing, resulting in a mighty example of God's sanctifying power. Once a healthy relationship is established, the merciful prophet remains deeply committed because of the balance previously eluded but now found. On a personal note the evidence of God and his powerful work in these men and women is miraculous and brings me joy to see. Even now writing this, faces of friends appear in my mind whose lives have been and are being transformed with these two gifts.

Looking elsewhere on the Urgency/Rapport Matrix, prophecy creates tension where either urgency or rapport is threatened by the immediate needs around righteousness and truth. The uncompromising foundation of this gift then tugs against most traits left of the center axis for urgency. Low-assertive people don't want to push and extend themselves, but prophets do. People with lower scores on the attitude scale are skeptical, wanting proof, but the prophet knows the truth and wants to proclaim it. Both of these traits—low assertive and low attitude—combined with prophecy require individuals to seek God and have him teach them to use these opposing forces to be more Christlike.

Finally, in the upper-left quadrant of the matrix we have representation of low scores for decisiveness, judgment, accommodating, and independence. Each of these exhibits a behavior that does not share the same sense of urgency as prophecy and therefore can create internal tension with two sides of our personality warring. People who score low in decisiveness desire to investigate and want time to decide, while the prophet knows and is ready to speak. The people who have lower results in accommodating want to blend in, be team players, not rock the boat; whereas prophets were made to rock the boat. Lower scores on the judgment scale favor an emotional response and movement from the heart; the prophet is Joe Friday, just the facts, righteousness, and the polarity created with a low sense of urgency pulls between the head and heart. Finally, people with low-independence behavior tend to be followers, flexible by nature to group thinking, and by now we understand this is not the starting point for a prophet.

Teaching

The person with teaching as primary will have internal conflict with gifts and traits higher on the urgency axis. Teaching as a gift leads a person to want to make sure the listener gets it, the source data, how the teacher arrived at the hypothesis, the implications and knowledge this entire process brings to them personally. The point is there is a painstaking process, and the teacher is willing to endure this so you do get it. But when we combine this with traits and gifts to the right of center with a increased sense of urgency and desire to act a tension arises; the moderating effect can be shorten the teaching process or slow the high urgency trait or gift so greater learning transpires.

Leadership

Leadership and service were discussed in chapter 9, where we looked at an entire movement in leadership thinking called servant leadership. While this leadership model is extremely important in our culture, these two gifts operating together as the dominant gifts can also give rise to tension. Those with the leadership-service combination have both gifts poised to take action, but serving is in the background and leadership wants to be up front and visible; thus, the tension is in the visibility and method of service. You may feel only a mild tension all the way up to a neurosis level. The way forward is understanding when to alter your approach. Your gifting means you possess a great ability, like a baseball switch hitter: if there is an advantage standing at the plate as a right hand hitter, do it, or if it is better as a lefty, you have that option too. God wired you this way; so your purpose is found in exercising this ability with God.

High Urgency, High Rapport

The other traits with a strong sense of urgency and greater need for rapport, located in the upper right quadrant, including energy, accommodating, extroverts, assertiveness, and attitude. These are all traits that will find tension where the uncertainty of beliefs, need to stand alone, or doubts from other traits creep into the mix. Remember, people with high energy are the ultimate multitaskers, whereas someone who is low decisive is more singularly focused; if someone's trait is low independence, they have a preference for being told what to do, whereas high-energy people have an endless list of things to do now. Our important take away is where some other gift or traits sacrifices rapport or urgency from how our natural response would be displayed in our behavior, tension can arise.

Low Urgency, Low Rapport

In the lower-left quadrant are those areas that share less regard for rapport and urgency. This includes low scores for assertiveness, attitude, energy, and sociability—for example, teaching, which we've already touched on, and high manageability, which we will discuss in a moment. People with low scores in attitude are more curious and suspicious, thus liking more time to explore, which includes any of the traits favoring action, proclamation of truth, taking charge now. Being less focused or competitive will create the discords we've been discussing. Low assertiveness displays in people with a greater sense of letting someone else decide, but internally these people will be torn if they also are strong in other traits or gifts such as attitude. The interesting one within this quadrant is high manageability where a person likes structure, being told more or given well-outlined processes, but will experience discord when ambiguity is present. That could be someone high in focus, from the upper-right quadrant, but also just as easily, tension can arise with traits and gifts low in both urgency and rapport, which are present in the same quadrant.

To live into our purpose with these points of discord, we should begin with self-awareness and our relationship with God as the foundation for transformation. Whether that begins with examining your Call results, some self awareness you previously had or God's revelatory work in your life, all truth is God's. So if you gain new awareness of points of tension, ask God to help you navigate them; after all, he knew about them when you were made. As with everything we have talked about regarding coaching and seeking God about the areas we're learning about, we can ask him to reveal the areas we don't understand, especially where we have some vague notion of discord, and coaching can be very useful and used by God as well. This is where fearlessness comes in: it self-examination and transformation were easy and could be done alone, we would all be doing it. Just another example of everyone playing their parts in the ensemble.

Those with lower sociability results, for example, will be introverted, thus inclined to be alone versus loving bolder social settings, being emotionally recharged by being quiet and alone. Discord happens for them when they are with other people and sharing truth or being confrontational. This is a great example where I love watching the sanctifying power of God. The introverted prophet wrestles with the bold proclamation of truth that they have inside. Without self-knowledge or the transformational power of God, it can well up, and when it is finally blurted out, sometimes it's looks like Old Faithful. The steam shoots high into the air and can burn everyone in vicinity. God absolutely loves this combination, not for the steam shooting in the air but because in submission to him, with the natural, thoughtful and deliberate approach of the introvert combined with knowledge of truth from the prophet, people are changed forever, and the truth will set them free. Whew, I get goose bumps watching this play out.

Let's shift gears to close out our discussion on discord. We've looked at the different quadrants of the Urgency/Rapport Matrix, examined some of, but intentionally not all, of the combinations of gifts and traits. It is worth mentioning that rarely do just two of these create either alignment or discord; most often it is several of these gifts and traits coming together in us, sometimes even quietly in the background, and then some situation triggers activation.

Let's ask God deeper into our discussion by praying; "God, show me the statements and agreements I make that keep you out, that lock you out in the cold and prevent me from living in fullness of who you want me to be. Please shine your light into those corners in my life and transform me. When these conflicts in my gifts and traits arise, show me what you would have me do. And above all, teach me to be like Jesus, not just to do what I think he'd do but to be transformed like him by your power and presence."

CHAPTER 11

The Way to Transformation

A LONG TIME AGO, while taking a manufacturing management class in college, I had the opportunity to do metal castings. It is truly a fascinating process. Beginning with a crucible, the metal is heated until the random chunks of aluminum begin to melt like ice cubes in a glass of water on a hot summer day—a bit hotter actually since aluminum becomes molten above 660 degrees Celsius. Only as the metal melts do the impurities separate; all the debris, pollutants, and contaminants that prevent the metal from being pure rise to the top. Whether it is gold, aluminum, steel, or some alloy, the process is similar and repeatable. This is the first step, and then the impurities are removed, scraped off the top of the crucible. This can't happen when the metal is cold or solid; it takes the heat of the crucible to release what is to be removed so that only a pure material is left behind.

Suffering is the crucible of our faith. Let's examine how this played out in the life of Jesus and then discover the wisdom from his example. Hebrews 5:7–9 says, "During the days of Jesus' life on earth, he offered up prayers and petitions with fervent cries and tears to the one who could save him from death, and he was heard because of his reverent submission. Son though he was, he learned obedience from what he suffered and, once made perfect, he became the source of eternal salvation for all who obey him." This is a rich passage. Throughout all the gospel stories Jesus is often praying, and we see the results: people are healed, restored, even raised from the dead. This was because of Jesus' "reverent submission." In John 15:7, Jesus tells us, "If you remain in me and my words remain in you, ask whatever you wish, and it will be done for you." Jesus exemplified obedience, the suffering servant, submission, continually seeking his Father, and a life laid down to his Father.

Later Jesus prays in the garden to find another way forward without a crucifixion. He asks God if there is another way to save the world. It is clear in the prior Hebrew passage and the gospel accounts overall that God listened to Jesus, like every other prayer, and heard his Son because of his faithful submission. Did God answer Jesus' prayer in the garden with a way out of the crucifixion? No, he didn't remove this suffering; this was the only way forward. Jesus suffered the excruciating pain of the cross, and his suffering made him alone the perfect sacrifice so you and I can be made perfect.

Now, I am not a theologian—you may have already figured that out—but Luke 2:52 also tells us, "Jesus grew in wisdom and stature, and in favor with God and man." God is transforming us into the form of his Son. More astounding to me is God's perfect Son was transformed this way as well. Why would Jesus need transformation? In honesty before someone sneaks in here saying that Jesus wasn't perfect, I am NOT saying that. He was perfect at the foundation of the world, during his time on earth, and after his resurrection. Scripture says in Hebrews 13:8 that "Jesus Christ is the same yesterday and today and forever," and in my heart I know this is true. But Jesus who was perfection was also growing, changing, and becoming "perfecter." My brain begins to cramp the moment two apparently mutually exclusive ideas exist in the same space and time.

Jesus was a lifelong learner, and I guess he still is; that alone is an intriguing thought. But he grew like you and I, though minus the fits and starts in our lives. This is remarkable: Jesus, the Son of God, was being transformed; he was learning and growing. You don't need to be a theologian to take comfort in the fact that Jesus set us a course for this life. Let it be said of us, too, that we grow "in wisdom and stature, and in favor with God and man." My mind is racing at the prospect that our perfect Savior was being made even more perfect, and the next question is, where is this trailhead for the journey of transformation?

One of the wonders of living in Colorado are the opportunities for hiking, biking, and paddling with the backdrop of some spectacular scenery. Being a lover of these wild places, when I hear someone share stories or see pictures of their extraordinary adventures, my first response is, "Where is that trailhead, and how can I get there?" Jesus has found the trailhead for personal transformation and it changes everything. The trail is marked with suffering. It is the crucible that provides the heat necessary to separate the impurities so they can be removed.

Looking at New Testament authors, we see a few other truths bubble up. Paul says in Philippians 3:10–11 (MSG), "I gave up all that inferior stuff so I could know Christ personally, experience his resurrection power, be a partner in his suffering, and go all the way with him to death itself. If there was any way to get in on the resurrection from the dead, I wanted to do it." Paul cashed it all in at the trailhead! Besides the power released by God for our transformation that works in us through suffering, we also see another reason in 2 Corinthians 1:4–6 (MSG): "He comes alongside us when we go through hard times, and before you know it, he brings us alongside someone else who is going through hard times so that we can be there for that person just as God was there for us. . . . When we suffer for Jesus, it works out for your healing and salvation." Your suffering and my suffering benefits each of us; we are comforted by God ourselves, but also he provides the wisdom and understanding to benefit those near us in the ensemble who are potentially walking in identical footsteps.

It seems so unfitting that in a discussion of suffering I would have used the word *benefit* twice. So many points of suffering appear unredeemable, senseless, unexplainable, or simply hurtful in a world of hurtfulness and hurting people. Some may know of Jesus, be a follower, and agree in faith that there are benefits that come from suffering. However, we can't just gloss over suffering, and it wouldn't be honest to ignore those who have no knowledge of Jesus or perhaps even more those who once expressed faith in him but have left Jesus because of suffering.

For a moment, if we return to Tao's story of the Chinese farmer, one can imagine his son suffered on some level when he broke his leg. The farmer didn't focus on his son's discomfort; there was only a wait and see what the new future would bring. "Maybe" was his chorus, and in our lives we need to hold things the same way. Believe me, this is significantly easier said than done.

Several years ago Marcie experienced a series of health crises, well beyond the normal challenges we'd grown accustomed to for almost twenty years prior, ending up with an incurable neurological condition. Life altering and gradually consuming both of us, she moved from a life of independence and self-motivated mobility to dependence on me for the simplest activities. My business screeched to a halt, and life moved to full-time caregiving—cooking and cleaning and frequent running to hospitals and doctor appointments. Marcie dealt with completely debilitating pain, rounds of physical therapy to overcome the pain, and further injury from falls. This was a roller coaster ride, each of us uniquely experiencing ups and downs in our own worlds all while traveling on this less-than-a-thrill ride together. To say "maybe" in the midst of this would have been ludicrous.

The reality is we were in survival mode for over fifteen months, and when one crisis ended, another started with a diagnosis of cancer. Where would this end? We didn't know. Would it end in death, was there redemption, was there transformation, to what end and purpose were these events unfolding? Frequently in the last twenty years I have equated Marcie's and my journey with the excruciating bushwhacks I led in my twenties guiding mountaineering trips in the Adirondack wilderness. All too often these would take us into pine thickets where trees grew only feet apart with branches interlocking. It was often like walking through a giant hairbrush, and in some instances it would be hours or days where we couldn't even look up or see the sky and sun. How do we fight our way through these times in life? In the midst of these crucible moments even the farmer's "maybe" escapes us. Not only are we entirely unsure of the way forward, but we haven't the foggiest idea what fruit the suffering will bring. Lamenting this at one point in my life, I had a friend share Psalm 119:105 with me: "Your word is a lamp for my feet, a light on my path." The author, whether it was David or Daniel, got it; he was unable to see the sky or the sun either because of the difficulty of his trail. Typically during those mountaineering trips, we were holding our heads down in the bushwhack, forcing our way through the branches. The head-down position was a must just to prevent the branches from literally scratching our eyes out, and it was dark, but just like the difficult moments in our lives, God's Word can light up our feet and the path, and the way forward is following this light.

So "maybe" is as good as it gets on those days, and sometimes we can't even muster that "maybe," but we move one foot forward at a time, right foot then left foot. My wife and I did; David, Jesus, and many before us did likewise; and while many times none of us could see the sky, following the light on the path was the way. We weren't writing a story on these days; the pen wasn't in our hand. Suffering had replaced it, but God's bigger story was still being recorded. The redemption work of God means it is shared today and points back to him. Today God's redemptive work can point back to the example of Jesus' suffering explained in Hebrews 5. Even Jesus, God's own Son, had to suffer, and through his obedience we are made perfect. Tim Keller points out the fundamental difference between being a follower of Jesus and following other religions when it comes to suffering: "Christianity teaches that, contra fatalism, suffering is overwhelming; contra Buddhism, suffering is real; contra karma, suffering is often unfair; but contra secularism, suffering is meaningful. There is a purpose to it, and if faced rightly, it can drive us like a nail deep into the love of God and into more stability and spiritual power than you can imagine."[1]

The work of God's transformation for our lives often takes place in the crucible of suffering. This makes us more fearless and able to have a greater connection with our purpose and significance.

CHAPTER 12

Special Needs
and Cognitive Challenges

IT IS IMPERATIVE TO include a chapter dedicated to those of us who don't test well, perhaps have challenges reading or barriers to an online assessment, or in general don't fit the clean bell-shaped curves we all strive to squeeze into. This is imperative when we are considering our purpose and significance in God's story. This chapter is borne from experience in life, business, and church with individuals who have been previously or still are excluded from the world of work or marginalized in some other fashion. These amazing individuals have been a pleasure to know and work beside. While much of what we've considered thus far was based on assessments that often don't work with this population, we need other frameworks and constructs.

Before we get practical, there is no better story to illustrate everyone's significance and purpose than the story of Josh. Josh's parents, dear friends of Marcie's and mine, have been in ministry with teens for twenty-five-plus years, and often they are the first called or woken when one of their families experiences a tragedy. Now in the words of Peggy, Josh's mom, "One never gets used to those calls in the evening alerting you to a tragedy. On a cold day in late January, my husband received a call on a Friday from a local police officer, using one of our former youth members' phone. The police asked if Joe would come immediately to their home, as one of the sons in their family had died. There are four sons in this family, with one of them already 'dead' at a young age. Joe hopped in the car and left quickly, asking Josh and me to pray for him and the family."

Peggy and Josh were just heading out to a prayer meeting in preparation for a Holy Spirit conference their church was hosting the following Saturday. Josh has already been recognized as a prayer warrior gifted with insights all the rest of us can only imagine. Peggy goes on, "As we typically do, I asked my son Josh to join me in praying for his dad and this family, whom Josh doesn't really know. I prayed for wisdom and compassion for Joe to walk with them in their loss."

Then Josh started to pray asking God to be with his dad, and Peggy said, "He just suddenly stopped." Peggy shared how Josh "seemed to be in communication with God and started saying, 'Yes, okay, I see.' He then began talking to God out loud, thanking him for caring for this man. 'Yes, Jesus,' he began, 'thank you for coming to the woods and scooping him up off the ground, and carrying him to God's lap.'" With this Josh turned to his mom and said, "He is okay now, because he's in God's lap."

This is an amazing story for anyone, but it's made just a bit more extraordinary as God makes the point of Josh's significant and purpose. You see, Josh, according to his mom, "is developmentally disabled, with a diagnosis of Fragile X. He is on the autism spectrum." Peggy has often commented, "We heard what Josh couldn't do. He could not comprehend many things academically, but he always had a sense about people and their hearts."

While Peggy's experience in the car was so special to her, it wasn't the end of the story. Joe, Josh's dad, listened to the family as the father shared how "their young twenty-four-year-old son [was] struggling with depression, and he had taken his life in the woods, near their home. The police found him on the ground, in the woods." Peggy's heart jumped. Josh had seen it all in his talk with the Lord. No question about it. Neither Peggy nor Josh knew the details about what had happened—except what Jesus told Josh, words Josh's father shared with the family, and it was a miracle to them as they deeply grieved the loss of a son. Peggy went on to say, "We have always thought Josh had a connection with the Lord, and that his communication was unlike any we had seen. Josh tunes in to the Lord in ways I can only hope to do." These are words of truth revealing a relationship with Jesus I want.

Therefore, what was said earlier specific to assessments needs to be considered differently when we are talking about people with special needs. We can't just give someone with special needs an online assessment and draw the same conclusion we've been examining so far in this book. The approach needs to incorporate creating workplace simulations and trials, interviewing people, and trying different things on. There is no assessment for Josh's experience that evening in prayer; we can't just read this account and determine his gifts and traits. We have to be living life out with someone, use an interview process, perhaps use a physical test or a combination of these in order to reveal their spiritual gifts, interest, and traits. Josh's story and the ones to follow aren't meant to make heroes of anyone; they are intended to be hopeful, challenging opportunities for cultural growth and encouragement for inclusion of everyone. There is still so much work to be done, and the heroes will be the people willing to take additional steps to include everyone because they are significant.

We must begin with the individual and get their story, their likes, things that energize them. It can be dreary work, paying close attention to specific cues, abilities, and cognitive strengths and barriers. This can be done by the individual and with family members, trained job coaches and caseworkers, and other professionals familiar with job skills, a particular job, and adaptability options. As the leader taking the initiative to find a place for someone or drive change, some creativity and thinking outside the box can go a long way.

Combining these ingredients then should progress into a few different trials and test runs where real life work is done and you, the individual and team, are assessing the situation. Everything from comprehension to focus and dexterity come into play. So a few real-life examples will be helpful here.

First was an individual who could neither hear nor speak. It took a number of iterations and trials to determine that his visual perception was exceptional, so his accuracy doing an assembly where placement of one part with precision onto another was critical and something he excelled at. Furthermore, because finding meaningful work and contribution had evaded him for so long, he could perform this repetitive task for long periods of time and without the natural decline in performance a traditional worker would experience because of lack of focus. He was actually very thrilled to outperform me, and his ability to contribute "altered his entire life," as a family member explained.

Another example shocked me when it took place. A young man received trade training for something I had no doubt he would excel at doing; however, without work experience he was denied the chance to use his training. In order to get him work experience, his caseworker approached me looking to our start-up to hire folks with cognitive disabilities. This individual was high functioning on the autism spectrum. I spent time doing workplace simulations, some simple work-related activities and various exercises to determine capability and fit. Manual dexterity immediately sunk to the bottom of skills, but an eye toward patterns in data emerged that resulted in the compliment, "You are a rock star at this." So a bit of creativity revealed one activity that was this individual's starting point. From this one starting point his experiences grew until he had a resume and went to work in his targeted trade. The foothold in the ensemble for a special needs individual begins like this.

Dozens of individuals I have worked alongside have had physical barriers, cognitive challenges, or behavioral biases that made one type of work impossible but another right up their alley. Paramount to finding a fit is communication, trial and error, setting up experiments, and working alongside individuals. Here are a few other considerations.

Readiness of the workplace is one consideration. New considerations enter the facility discussion that never needed addressing before. In the case of new buildings, the Americans with Disabilities Act (ADA) addresses some of the physical items, which can include ramps, remote access doors, restrooms, break rooms, and dining areas as well as potential work cell/space items. However, even in the best of situations other modifications or accommodations may be necessary specific to the work, and in the case of older buildings additional measures may also be necessary. These are good to walk through, piece by piece, and to document. Emergency egress was something I never thought of, but in one building I observed, two exits had stairs outside that meant alternatives or modifications were required. The young man in our first example who neither could speak or hear required that we have lights and sirens for fire and emergency. Having a whole team of people at one facility required no costly modification, just a thoughtful and intentional conversation, a plan, and testing.

The existing associate population likewise needs to assess their readiness, and the best approach is proactive communications, training, and policies for dealing with questions as they arise. Beginning with team training was incredibly helpful for our startup project. As a proponent of culture, the benefits of associates being proud of where they worked as a result of our outreach meant they were willing to make accommodations, and it elevated the entire team's performance. Making sure there is compatibility between current workplace policies and any new or inclusive populations is important. Broadening the discussion of diversity, for example, to include newer views, like cognitive diversity, was also helpful. In these forums people can ask questions and get clarity around how to interact and support one another.

Easterseals, Goodwill, state-managed vocational rehabilitation, work placement programs, and community leaders are a few areas with potential support for your efforts of advancing opportunities and inclusion of a vital part of the ensemble with the goal of helping everyone realize their purpose and significance. You will find other resources and success stories online at www.rickadlerandassociates.com/fearlesspurposeandsignificance.

CHAPTER 13

Living in Purpose
and Significance Today

PARTLY BECAUSE OF VOCATION and partly because of predisposition, words, ideas, and thoughts must be harnessed and joined to be useful in life. Being a wealth of useless information seems only to serve you if you are a contestant on *Jeopardy* or playing Trivia Pursuit, but real life requires *useful* information. Perhaps the idea that everything must be useful is too utilitarian or is thinking too hard but I am hopeful. There is a necessity that the pages and truth preceding this chapter draw you fearlessly into your purpose and significance in God's story.

Ultimately, we are the created, not the Creator, and therefore are here at the good pleasure of God. Being here at his good pleasure means what Paul says in Romans 12:1–2 (MSG):

So here's what I want you to do, God helping you: Take your everyday, ordinary life—your sleeping, eating, going-to-work, and walking-around life—and place it before God as an offering. Embracing what God does for you is the best thing you can do for him. Don't become so well-adjusted to your culture that you fit into it without even thinking. Instead, fix your attention on God. You'll be changed from the inside out. Readily recognize what he wants from you, and quickly respond to it. Unlike the culture around you, always dragging you down to its level of immaturity, God brings the best out of you, develops well-formed maturity in you.

Let's walk backward through this passage. God desires to bring out your best, which is your testimony to the culture. We do that by fixing our attention on God. Because of all God has done, the reasonable response is to offer our lives as a sacrifice. This means we should do everything in every moment for God. From Romans 1 through Romans 11 Paul shares what God has done for all of humankind. Most of Paul's writing is done in a structure call indicative and imperatives. Paul explains something God has done and then we find a "therefore" or "but;" some wind up like a pitcher on the mound; Paul's pitch is what we should do. Technically it means because God did this, it is "reasonable," or "we ought to respond this way."

So Romans 11:36 sums it up well: "For from him and through him and for him are all things." It's all about God, which is reassuring when I look at the big wide world.

The "therefore" is Romans 12:1 above, we should offer our whole life as a living sacrifice to God, to enter into the ensemble and be a part of his story because of everything God has done for us. God doesn't make it hard, we do our everyday lives in service to him.

So again, it's his story, and our part today begins where we are at this very moment. Meanwhile God is moving. He is able to move through history and into the future, never bound as we are. Instead, one moment he is busy creating, redeeming, and writing the chapters that have led to where we find ourselves today, and in the next moment he is busy working way upstream. Like the Israelites crossing the Jordan River when the water stopped only as their foot entered the water's edge, today we may have a chance encounter for coffee with a friend that becomes a sacrifice of love, or we may receive a call that a deal is done or won't come through; let's watch and anticipate what God will reveal as we enter the river and see the water stop.

First and foremost, then, where are you in your relationship with God, Jesus, and the Holy Spirit? In the event this is the first you've considered a God who not only cares about you and the world but also, more importantly and powerfully, loves you and believes you are significant then there is the question. What about the fact that God has a plan for you, God devised an amazing plan, and it began with his Son, Jesus, who died for you, me, and all people, but he thinks we're worth it. Not only that but the story isn't finished, and he has a place for you in the ensemble and in his story. Do you want to be in on the biggest story ever written? Then start by asking God to take control of your life, trust God who had his Son die for you. "Sincy" was my dad's way to tell the kindergarten-me, "It is really simple." God showed us how significant we all are by the price he was willing to pay. Now we are taking another step with him because he wants us involved with his story. Pray with me now: "Jesus, I am so thankful you died for me, for my sins, and that you've shown me how much you love me. Show me more, become more real, and energize my life and show me how to be a part of your ensemble."

That's a great start. You don't need to quit smoking or swearing or whatever else you might name as your sins; eventually Jesus may want you to part company with those habits. I did with the first, not so much the second, but regardless, that isn't the starting point. You've taken the first step if you prayed that simple two-sentence prayer above. What is helpful is to get connected and tell someone, but first ask God to open those doors. It could be scary, churches can be scary, and church people can be scarier. I know, I'm one of them, but remember, unlike Jesus, you and I aren't perfect yet, and that is why it's scary. Ask God anyway to help you and lead you fearlessly. Resources and contact

information are available at www.rickadlerandassociates.
com/fearlesspurposeandsignificance.

It is worth mentioning at this point that in every
story that has a good, loving, and benevolent hero,
there is also an evil villain desiring to undo the good, to
enslave the characters, and to wreak havoc. Sometimes
these villains are simply what James McClendon calls the
"tournament of narratives."[1] Recently a blog post from
the Ransomed Heart ministry, John Eldridge's online
presence, summarized these opposing forces this way:
"In our culture," sin, distraction, additions, or merely the
stories and agreements we've made up, "there is a clash
of many small dramas competing for our heart. Through
baseball and politics and music and sex and even church,
we are searching desperately for a Larger Story in which to
live and find our role."[2]

At some points in our lives we may suffer a frontal
attack from Satan himself: a bold knock on the front door
followed by some trauma, disease, or disaster. Other times
it's a diversion from the same villain; we just don't notice
the attack because of the subtlety. In these moments some
smaller stories entice us, offering counterfeit flavors and
experiences, and because we lose hope and faith easily, we
sell out the bigger story for the immediate gratification—
not unlike the brother in the Bible who sold his birthright
for a bowl of soup, Genesis 27. Guard your heart and seek
God for clarity and revelation about where these pieces
might be enticing you.

Now, let's pretend we got married today, had been courting for a while, as they used to say, but just got hitched today. Well, the next step isn't to rush off and pour ourselves into becoming a world-renowned neurosurgeon. Let's get our marriage off on the right foot, have a honeymoon, and figure out a bit of life together. Life with Jesus is the same. After your first day following him, maybe in the next few weeks or months you can press into what God might have as the next step. Maybe the next step is taking The CALL online, but finding a church and other Christians around you is actually more pressing.

Perhaps you picked up the book because you sense yours is a life in transition and were hopeful the pages would provide some insight. Maybe you've been a follower of Jesus and just sense it is time to begin a career that serves him. Or maybe the first half of your life has been focused on success and you want the second to shift to significance. There are also folks out there right now who gave up on the story a long time ago. Perhaps your age has caught up with you, life has worn you down, or the state of the world or modern politics has cast doubt on a love story being written. You are in luck: this is your call back into the story. To write a chapter God has just for you. Maybe some younger person needs a sage re-entering the battle to mentor and lead them. Perhaps you are an author with a story he's given you. Maybe your part is to reshape your community, business, or church. Just maybe, if you don't give up, maybe you still have arrows in your quiver, and God is calling to use it for his story.

Or maybe your life is right on track—career, marriage, stock portfolio are all trending precisely the way you planned—and this was just an intriguing title or read. Sorry, but Jesus tends to break into stories, and now God is whispering, and your decision to listen carefully could change everything. I am excited for you, a little nervous, but mostly hopeful to have you in the ensemble.

So where are you in life, vocationally, relationally, with regard to health, financial resources, or any of life's situations? We can also speak to the fact that sometimes none of these matter, and instead some big hairy audacious goal (BHAG) that we have is the driver of our life plan. Then suddenly our BHAG is disrupted by a big hairy audacious God who just played the highest trump card in the deck and our goal is replace by God. BHAG becomes a big hairy audacious God. And oh how sweet it is to follow the author of history into the story, to be in the ensemble, and to thrive in our part.

I love that Jesus doesn't want us to do a bunch of things and doesn't have some formula for success. It isn't about religion; it is about relationship with Jesus, our everyday life lived with him. Earlier I shared Matthew 11:28–30 (msg): "Are you tired? Worn out? Burned out on religion? Come to me. Get away with me and you'll recover your life. I'll show you how to take a real rest. Walk with me and work with me—watch how I do it. Learn the unforced rhythms of grace. I won't lay anything heavy or ill-fitting on you. Keep company with me and you'll learn to live freely and lightly." We only need to walk and work with him, watch him, have Jesus teach us rhythms, to live freely, to rest, and to walk lightly.

Everyone you choose to let in on how God wants to transform you should sound like Jesus; they should not lay anything heavy or ill-fitting on you. As I described earlier, suffering is the crucible and will come, but you don't need to go find heaviness, poor-fitting situations, or people who may think they are special and hence uniquely qualified to tell you what to do. As I was reflecting on how to wrap this up, I confessed one morning to a group of brothers that you should hold my words as Jesus would have you hold them. Some words God will whisper and say about them, "Yes, you should listen." Where you push against what I said and ask God and you still aren't sure, pray that Jesus brings clarity, and where I was off, pray that you'd forget those words. The great story of God is a secret mission; as 1 Corinthians 2:7 (TPT) puts it, "Instead, we continually speak of this wonderful wisdom that comes from God, hidden before now in a mystery. It is his secret plan, destined before the ages, to bring us into glory." Ann Voskamp, in *One Thousand Gifts*, decodes the secret mission this way: "He means to rename us—to return us to our true names, our truest selves. He means to heal our soul holes. From the beginning, that Eden beginning, that has always been and always is, to this day. His secret purpose—our return to full glory."

What you choose to do next matters greatly and matters not at all. It is God's story. He's told us the end and knows every page in between, and believe me no editor will rewrite what God has to say, so it doesn't matter. But what you do matters greatly because you are needed in the story today to be a part of the ensemble. I also want to rub elbows with you; you are gifted, fearless, uniquely wired, and significant.

CHAPTER 14

Living in Purpose
and Significance with Others

WELCOME TO THE ENSEMBLE. We would be amiss if we didn't spend some time discussing what God would have us know about the ensemble, how we are to interact, what to do when the wheels fall off life or if we simply lose our way, and useful ways to fully live in this larger context and play out our part in the ensemble. Let's start with Paul who puts it this way in Ephesians 2:20–22 (MSG): "He used the apostles and prophets for the foundation. Now he's using you, fitting you in brick by brick, stone by stone, with Christ Jesus as the cornerstone that holds all the parts together. We see it taking shape day after day—a holy temple built by God, all of us built into it, a temple in which God is quite at home."

This is but one of Paul's many pictures of the ensemble, and a beautiful one indeed, because many of us have tried the Christian walk on our own and it hasn't worked out so well. We also find we are lacking key elements, traits, and gifts that can only be met when we join one another. Another example pulled from Paul is worthy of examining. In Ephesians 6 he brings up the picture of a Roman soldier's armor—not a surprising metaphor since Paul at the time was chained to one 24/7, all the while thinking of God and words of encouragement for saints, both in his time and for the ages to come. Paul talks of the spiritual equipment all warriors need, but perhaps the ploy of Roman military strategists not portrayed is the greatest weapon—the mandible, sometimes also called the tortoise formation.

Entering into battle this formation could support horses and chariots riding across the top and could drive back the opposition even when vastly outnumbered, as one scene in the movie *300* so graphically portrayed. This formation was demoralizing to an enemy trying to attack. Not unlike a dog attacking a tortoise, there is no real way to get at the dang thing. Here the ensemble's formation is intended to maximize damage to the opponent and withstand overwhelming odds.

In formation those on the edges used swords and in the middle longer spears called pikes to reach out at the enemy. Shields were interlocked so that arrows dropping from the sky would bounce off like water on a turtle's shell. The point of this is the ensemble is facing a daunting foe. While Jesus has already laid claim to the victory in Ephesians 6, Paul reminds us our enemy is shooting live ammo. Stay long enough on this earth and walk with Jesus, and you'll see folks taken out. This is a battle, and while the gifts you and I bring to God's story are vital, I honestly also like having the company of other warriors when I'm facing a good battle. It's not a bad idea either to have another shield interlocked with mine, someone jabbing a pike from over my shoulder at those battling against me, and the company of those whose gifts I can't live without.

Right in the context of Paul discussing gifts, the very ones we've been examining from Romans 12:5 (MSG), he shares this: "So since we find ourselves fashioned into all these excellently formed and marvelously functioning parts in Christ's body, let's just go ahead and be what we were made to be, without enviously or pridefully comparing ourselves with each other, or trying to be something we aren't." This book is built on several key concepts that relate directly to how we relate as individuals. We are significant, each of us, and without you alongside me and vice versa, the form is less "excellent" and "marvelous." We are encouraged by Paul, encouragement being one of Paul's gifts, to "be what we were made to be," not something we aren't. At minimum in this mission we will want someone really strong there next to us; we'll each bring something this mission requires. Finally, let's remember that God has others ready to enter the story at our side, and we don't want to toss anyone aside that he has called and made.

Our brother Peter also shares some of God's view in 1 Peter 2:5 (MSG): "Present yourselves as building stones for the construction of a sanctuary vibrant with life, in which you'll serve as holy priests offering Christ-approved lives up to God." We have a choice every day to present ourselves. Here Peter is talking of a splendid sanctuary, a refuge, teaming and vibrant with life. Do we want to be a part of this structure offering refuge and life as holy priests of Christ? Wow, that's a pretty cool part to play, and we are all priests; none of us is the high priest—that would be Christ—but in this sanctuary I'm not just lighting the candles before the service either. God has us serving it up in Christ. My actions here aren't about works, earning my way or somehow qualifying myself through what I do. Your choice, you in or out?

Old labels and identities are gone too. Simon is now Peter, vacillator to the Rock. If you grew up being known as wimpy, klutzy, ugly, dumb, wishy-washy, wouldn't you like a name change? Heck yeah, some of those names hit pretty close to home for me, but Paul says, "The old labels we once used to identify ourselves—labels like Jew or Greek, slave or free"—insert your own, could be names of pride too—"are no longer useful. We need something larger, more comprehensive. I want you to think about how all this makes you more significant, not less. A body isn't just a single part blown up into something huge. It's all the different-but-similar parts arranged and functioning together" (1 Corinthians 12:13–14 MSG). God has a new name for us, and he wants us to know we are even more significant than we think we are and there is a BIG part waiting from our big hairy audacious God.

It is in the midst of all these truths that our behavior should also be unique and different from the majority of our favorite sports teams or elected officials. In Colossians 3:12–15 Paul outlines the truth about us being "God's chosen people, holy and dearly loved," but because this is who we are we, we are to "clothe [ourselves] with compassion, kindness, humility, gentleness and patience. Bear with each other and forgive one another if any of you has a grievance against someone. Forgive as the Lord forgave you. And over all these virtues put on love, which binds them all together in perfect unity. Let the peace of Christ rule in your hearts, since as members of one body you were called to peace. And be thankful."

Before you get lost in my word gymnastics or quickly sweep this under a rug because you've heard it time after time, please stop and for just a moment visualize this: If I was a superhero, I'd wave my magic wand and everyone in the world would be compassionate, kind, humble, gentle, patient, loving, and unifying. What would happen then? Peace, thankfulness, gratitude, but also no starvation because we'd all share, no human trafficking because we'd all honor one another, no school violence because the marginalized and mentally ill would be loved and helped to wholeness and wellness.

If you are reading this and are a follower of Jesus, that is what we are supposed to represent, but if we're honest, often these qualities don't cross pews or rows on Sunday morning, let alone reach into our families or neighborhoods. When did your train and mine become unhitched in the middle of that passage? We must ask Jesus to show us where and help us work at letting the "peace of Christ rule in [our hearts]" so that we can change this place and make God's story even more inviting.

To allow the peace of Christ to rule our hearts and, as Peter tells us in 1 Peter 2:5 (MSG), to "present yourselves" requires that we are in the room. This is the idea of being present, living in the moment, or, to quote today's culture, practicing mindfulness. These passages neither allow us just to show up nor do they relegate any of us to be a benchwarmer. No benchwarmers on God's team or in the mandible. A benchwarmer is not someone I want to stand next to, do you? I also don't want to let the person next to me down either, so I need both of us to be present.

I earnestly believe Jesus was *always* in the moment, focused on precisely what the person or people in front of him needed, and always present with God. Being like Jesus, then, strikes me as the only way to focus one's awareness and calmly acknowledge what God would have me do for the ensemble. Christ offers me a unique and different point of view that is actually the way you and I were designed to work: moment my moment with Jesus, God, and the Holy Spirit our minds filled, overflowing with the presence of the trinity.

Finally, the commission that Paul sent to the Ephesians seems very fitting here. Ephesians 4:2–7 (MSG) says this:

> I want you to get out there and walk—better yet, run!—on the road God called you to travel. I don't want any of you sitting around on your hands. I don't want anyone strolling off, down some path that goes nowhere. And mark that you do this with humility and discipline—not in fits and starts, but steadily, pouring yourselves out for each other in acts of love, alert at noticing differences and quick at mending fences.
>
> You were all called to travel on the same road and in the same direction, so stay together, both outwardly and inwardly. You have one Master, one faith, one baptism, one God and Father of all, who rules over all, works through all, and is present in all. Everything you are and think and do is permeated with Oneness.
>
> But that doesn't mean you should all look and speak and act the same. Out of the generosity of Christ, each of us is given his own gift.

This is the type of picture Paul and God team up to create, one that is energizing, intentional and makes me want to live fearlessly with purpose and significance. This picture is much more fulfilling and works better with how you and I are wired. How different will God make the world by shaping us into this kind of ensemble? That is up to you and me and whether we choose to live fearlessly in purpose and significance!

Resources

https://rickadlerandassociates.com/fearlesspurposeandsignificance

You will find personal or small group questions for each chapter, current links to the websites below as well as other useful websites and resources. Contact information and information about partners supporting this book are also available.

Chapter 11 *The Way of Transformation*
Andy Stanley and North Point Ministries provide an insightful and encouraging series titled *In The Meantime*, on what to do when life takes a turn or when you are in transition or a place of suffering. These messages have been used powerfully in our lives during times of trial and are now part of our story. http://northpoint.org/messages/in-the-meantime/

Chapter 12 *Special Needs and Cognitive Challenges*
There are a number of resources listed below that I became familiar with during the process of writing this book. I am equally certain you know of others. I have

differing levels of experience with these and there are no guarantees implied, as most anyone who has experience personally or with loved ones with any type of disability or special need can attest to. The attempt is to simply share some of my findings to aid in some small part your navigating the tangled world of services, support, and resources for careers and life with any type of disability or special needs.

1. Steve Tonkin and Company - http://stevetonkin.com/ person-centered-planning/

This resource combines work on Person-centered planning for those with disabilities and a deep familiarity with The CALL.

Applies a unique approach of contextualizing and applying the (gifts) to help professional service agencies develop person-centered plans for individuals with Intellectual/Developmental Disabilities (I/DD) who receive home and community based services (HCBS) covered by Medicaid as required by the Centers for Medicare & Medicaid Services (CMS)

2. D.I.C.E.© - http://diceassessment.com

This resource is targeted for those primarily looking for vocational access that have some type of visible or invisible disability.

Bio - Denise Feltham is a person with an invisible disability who attained her bachelor of social work degree,

with Honors, from Ryerson University, a registered Social
Workers and Social Service Workers campus. She created
the rudimentary version of D.I.C.E.© (Disability Impact
on Career/Employment) during a field placement, Denise
pursued a Career and Work Counselor diploma from
George Brown College, and obtained her first job as a
vocational assessment and employment counselor with the
YWCA Youth Are program. She is a certified Life Skills
Coach and refined the D.I.C.E.© self-assessment tool
and her business 2008. Her latest addition to D.I.C.E.
Assessment & Employment Counseling Services is the
Life Skills for the World of Work series.

3. http://meantimeseries.org/wheres-your-focus
    Andy Jones with North Point Ministries shares his
family's story with autism and what it has meant to them.
An encouraging and real look at walking into their story
and seeing God at work.

Endnotes

Preface

1. W. E. Vine, M.A. *An Expository Dictionary of Net Testament Word; with their Precise Meanings for English Readers* (Old Tappan, N.J.: Revell, 1940), 232.

2. Os Guinness, *The Call: Finding and Fulfilling the Central Purpose of Your Life* (Nashville, TN: Thomas Nelson, 1998), 47.

3. "Interview: Max Lucado on Storytelling, the Church, and Politics," interview by Michelle A. Vu, www.christianpost. com, October 5, 2011, https://www.christianpost.com/ news/interview-max-lucado-on-storytelling-the-church-and-politics-57347/.

4. Erwin Raphael McManus. *The Last Arrow: Save Nothing for the Next Life* (Colorado Springs, CO: WaterBrook, 2017), 28.

Chapter 1

1. John Eldredge, *Beautiful Outlaw: Experiencing the Playful, Disruptive, Extravagant Personality of Jesus* (New York: FaithWords, 2011), 58.

2. John Eldredge, *Beautiful Outlaw* (New York: FaithWords, 2011), 137.

Chapter 2
1. Gallup and Tom Rath, *StrengthsFinder 2.0* (New York: Gallup Press, 2007).

Chapter 3
1. Martin Luther, *The Estate of Marriage* (1522), accessed May 11, 2018, https://brendenlink.wordpress.com/2013/03/09/luther-on-the-estate-of-marriage-1522/.

Chapter 4
1. "Special," *Oxford Living Dictionaries*, accessed May 10, 2018, https://en.oxforddictionaries.com/definition/special.

Chapter 5
1. Henri J. M. Nouwen, *A Cry for Mercy: Prayers from the Genesee* (New York: Doubleday, 1981).
2. Ashlee Pandley, *Academy Dictionary of Film, Television, and Theatre* (Adarsh Nagar, Dehli: Isha Books, 2005), 130.

Chapter 6
1. C. S. Lewis, *The Four Loves* (New York: HarperCollins, 1960), 73.
2. Randy Austad, *The CALL Vocational and Life Purpose Guide*, accessed April 12, 2010, www.FollowYourCalling.com, 2008, http://www.followyourcalling.com/thecall/sample%20call%20report.pdf.

Chapter 7
1. "Attitude," *Cambridge Dictionary*, accessed May 9, 2018, https://dictionary.cambridge.org/dictionary/english/attitude.

2. The parable of the Taoist farmer is estimated to have originated in approximately 500 BC.

3. Ann Voskamp, *One Thousand Gifts: A Dare to Life Fully Right Where You Are* (Grand Rapids, MI: Zondervan, 2010).

Chapter 8

1. "Rapport," *Oxford English Dictionary Online*, March 2018, Oxford University Press, accessed May 3, 2018, https://en.oxforddictionaries.com/definition/rapport.

Chapter 9

1. Robert K. Greenleaf, *The Servant as Leader* (Cambridge, MA: Center for Applied Science, 1970).

2. Robert K. Greenleaf, 7.

3. National Broadcasting Corporation. *Dragnet* (1951–59, 1967–70).

Chapter 11

1. Tim Keller, *Walking with God through Suffering and Pain* (New York: Penguin Books, 2013), 29.

Chapter 13

1. James McClendon, "Trapped in the Present," Ransomed Heart, February 15, 2018, https://ransomedheart.com/daily-reading/trapped-present.

2. James McClendon.